Dedication

To Anna, whose cheerful participation in my cruising dreams helped them to become reality, and without whose presence they might never have been fulfilled. Her social skills aboard, and her talents in the galley have spoiled the skipper and entertained a hundred guests in ways not expected on a small cruising boat. Thanks, honey. You've shared my lifelong dreams, my fears, and my delights—you've made it all worthwhile.

And to all the future cruiser, the folks just beginning to scheme and plan—it *IS* worth the time and effort to cruise. Because it can be the joyful highlight of your life's voyage. Just prepare carefully and take small steps until you're sure this is the direction you want to head. Then set a steady course to departure, and, without deviation, throw clear those dock lines that bind you to shore. It is my hope that this book will help you steer your boat to endless cruising delights and adventures, that you'll reach the landfalls of your fondest dreams.

All About Cruising

Credits

Cover Design - Sheriann Van Duren
Illustrator and Cartoonist - Sean Joseph Cahill
Photographers - Walt Gleckler, Anna Gleckler, Helen Brown, Elaine Eggum
Editors - Marty Campbell, Patricia Miller Rains, Christina Maule
Typesetting and Production - Point Loma Publishing

ISBN 0-9661416-3-6

Fully indexed & illustrated

Published by Passagemaker Productions
P.O. Box 359
Seal Beach, California 90740

1st printing January 1998

Boating/Cruising/Travel, Sailing, Outdoor/Marine, Retirement, Alternate Lifestyle

Printed in the United States of America

All About Cruising

Prepare Yourself

Equip Your Boat

Plan Your Escape

Live Your Dream

Walt Gleckler

Passagemaker Productions
Seal Beach, California
1998

All About Cruising

Acknowledgments

For daughter Sheriann, whose talent and artistic eye created the beautiful cover design used on *All About Cruising*. Through at least 30 different versions, she endured myriad suggestions and comments from family and friends—and always with patience and good humor. Much love, Sheri.

For Marty Campbell, good friend and editor, who labored mightily to unravel the author's fuzzy thoughts and to instill enough punctuation skill to clarify his twisted style—my deepest appreciation. Your patience and careful editing kept me on pace and focused throughout the long writing of this book.

For Sean Cahill, my 16-year-old illustrator and cartoonist, who is just beginning to discover his talents and abilities, my gratitude. Your devotion to my project is greatly appreciated. Your future is bright, indeed.

And for Marv Miller from the schooner "Endurance," and Jeff Thompson of the sloop "Victoria," many thanks for sharing details of your ship's medical kits and abandon-ship bags for inclusion in these pages.

About the Author

For most of his life, Walt Gleckler has been drawn to the sea—first in dinghies, and then for years of competitive sailing in keel boats. At some point he started to dream of distant shores and began the transformation into a cruising sailor. A sabbatical cruise to the South Pacific only whetted his appetite. He returned to teach at Orange Coast College in Southern California in the mid 1970s, and found a growing interest in the boating community for training in marine subjects. Eventually he developed a dozen different courses for boaters and cruisers.

For the past 23 years Walt Gleckler has coordinated the "Sailing Adventure Series" that brings well known cruising personalities to the college stage. During those years, Walt and his lovely wife Anna led more than a score of flotilla, charterboat cruises to international locations—from Greece to Australia. Retirement finds him even more active in boating activities. Only recently have the Glecklers returned from a five-year cruise aboard their 37' sloop "Passage."

All About Cruising

Contents

Foreword

For a long time I have felt there was a need for a book that lays out the steps that one must take to prepare for successful cruising—from the initial dream through vessel selection and preparation, to the attainment of necessary boating skills. Every person's approach to achieving these goals may be different, will proceed at a different pace, and will probably start from a different point. A large pool of essential information is common to all successful cruises, as is the development of expertise to sail and navigate ones own boat. All this information and skill must be acquired or mastered before departure. My hope is that this book will help you start—or continue—the process of voyage preparation that will lead you to fulfill your dreams.

The rewards can be life-long, and in the process, they'll change all your perspectives and priorities. The successful completion of a cruise by a boating couple is a memorable achievement, one that binds them together in ways not possible ashore. But the opposite can also be true if the cruise is not successful, so don't jump the gun. Dream, prepare, and depart. But do your homework first. Departure preparations can be one of the most challenging tasks you'll ever perform, but perhaps the rewards will be the greatest, too.

Walt Gleckler

Chapter 1

What Is Cruising?

Cruising Can Be Many Things

Cruising can be a weekend sail to your favorite anchorage across the bay, a trip up or down the coast to visit marinas and yacht clubs, a seasonal cruise to Mexico or the Bahamas, or an extended voyage lasting months or years. It can include coastal and offshore passages covering thousands of miles and touching many countries. All of these voyages may be considered "cruising," but the preparation for each subsequent step will become more extensive. Cruising can be as long as a weekend or last a lifetime. Many of the longer cruises fall into the 6-months to 3-year range. Lots of folks seem able to organize their lives and finances for this time period. They plan to then either return home, relocate, sell the boat, go back to work, retire, start planning for their next voyage, change partners, change boats – or any combination of the above.

Who Cruises?

People who decide to go cruising come from every walk of life, every profession, and every age group. There are many more boats "out there" today than there were just 10 years ago. Most are drawn by a dream to live a different, simpler lifestyle—uncluttered by many of societies' regimens and free from the hurried pace of their lives. Some are long-time boaters who move easily into the cruising style. Others

What it's all about.

are new to boating and theirs is a fast track into the nautical world. It really makes little difference, if you're a good learner and take little steps as you begin. At a minimum, give yourself several years to organize your cruising goals and make preparations. Just take your time until you are confident in your abilities and you know your vessel well.

People of all ages cruise. Many are in the 30- to 40-year age group. They are young and affluent enough to buy good and well equipped cruising boats. And they are positioned professionally to be able to take off for a 1- to 3-year sabbatical voyage. Entire families cruise, too—which require special planning and educational consideration.

Another large group is composed of retirees—older folk who have sometimes been dreaming and scheming for years, wanting to have a last fling at one of life's great and beautiful adventures. Of course there are also a few solo sailors of various ages and quite a few foreign cruisers, mostly French, British, German, New Zealanders, and Aussies. The majority of the boats are between 30 and 45 feet and are sailed by two persons—generally a man and a woman, although two men, two women, single handers (both men and women), and larger crews are common, too.

Powerboats are out here, too.

By far the largest percentage of cruisers at distant anchorages are sailors rather than powerboaters. However, more and more well-found powerboats are venturing long distances from home waters—even transoceanic. Recently a Nordhavn 46 from Dana Point,

California, completed a 4-year circumnavigation. She was powered by a single, 140 HP diesel engine with tankage for 1100 gallons. Seamanship is not limited to the heeling decks of sailboats, but can be seen in the most primitive native pangas as well as at the helm of passage-making powerboats. There seems to be a common bond that links those who are drawn to the sea in small craft and respect her traditions.

Why Cruise?

For most people, cruising represents a form of freedom and escape—from pressure- packed lives and high stress jobs, from personal lives that yearn for release and fulfillment, and from the encirclement and constraint of humanity. Many who have largely completed those things that society has thought (and elders have taught) to be socially responsible still yearn for something else: perhaps to live their own dream of personal freedom in harmony with nature and her natural laws—to sail and explore beyond the sunset.

South Pacific landfall.

The same force that led pioneers to drive west in covered wagons and rugged New Englanders to build and sail great clipper ships still lives in the recesses of many souls. It is a quest for adventure and discovery, a search for natural beauty and serenity, and a need for personal validation, accomplishment, and fulfillment. Although we are caught up in civilization's constant bombardment, modern men and women can often find harmony and contentment on the deck of their own small boat. In the preparation for cruising, we gain insight into the need for personal independence and self sufficiency of an earlier, simpler time—along with the growing realization that human kind and their dreams are much the same throughout the ages.

Cruising Dreams

Dare to dream. Much has been written about the ability of the subconscious mind to bring to fruition dreams and strongly held convictions. Working away in the background, the subconscious finds solutions to problems we cannot solve with conscious thought. Put this powerful force to work on your cruising dreams. Move beyond wishful thinking and start the 3-step departure process: begin purposeful dreaming, make a positive cruise plan, move on to a definite departure commitment.

I know of several cruisers who, months prior to their leaving, announced to friends and relatives the exact date and even the time they would leave on their long planned cruise. And in every case—it worked. They left as scheduled; one boat, even to the exact minute as announced months before! Perseverance to a positive cruising commitment made it happen just as they had originally dreamed and planned.

If you never establish your cruising goals in conscious thought, the subconscious cannot work on your behalf to find solutions for the myriad problems and roadblocks to fulfilling those dreams. Beware, lest you join the ranks of wishful thinkers who never leave the dock. Many now enjoying the cruising life had problems similar to your own: no boat, little money, no one to share their dream, job insecurities, kids in school, physical handicaps, no marine background, and on and on. Your commitment and perseverance will make the difference.

Cruising Goals

The goals of active cruisers may be quite different. Some say their desire to visit foreign countries and interact with native people is their aim, so they persue an immersion into culture and language. To others, it's experiencing the diversity of the earth's flora and fauna that counts. And for still more, just gaining release from the pressures and stress of modern society is the most important thing—to drop their hook in an emerald lagoon or sip a cool drink on a palm-fringed beach is what it's all about. Others like the challenge of getting there, the mechanics of steering, sailing, and navigating their own boat on a passage. Some gain satisfaction in the performance of a vessel that was built, modified, or improved with their own two hands. Many enjoy the warm clear tropical waters and attempt to supplement their diet with line and spear. But for most cruisers, it is probably a combination of things—perhaps including all or most of the above.

Where Do They Cruise?

Most U.S. cruisers are drawn to tropical waters for the bulk of their cruising, but by no means all. For the strong and adventurous, there is high-latitude sailing to satisfy even the most die-hard oceanic voyager. From all coasts of the U.S., the tropics are readily accessible to mom and pop cruisers in well-found vessels. From the West Coast, the tropical access is through Mexico, a most enjoyable detour. On the East Coast, the passage starts with the Bahamas—an equally pleasant diversion. Starting on the Gulf Coast, you're almost there when you begin your cruise. If you do decide to head north to the Canadian Maritimes, Canada, or Alaska, then your cruising will require more experience and certainly a well-equipped vessel. On passages far north or south, the chances are good that you could encounter more demanding weather and sea conditions than are found in more temperate climates. And should your goals be blue water—to cross oceans—then the Mediterranean and South Pacific beckon seductively.

How Long Do They Cruise?

Some cruises are open-ended. This is probably the ideal way to experience cruising as most of us envision it. A few long-term cruisers have arranged their personal lives and finances so they can stay out "as long as it's fun." Their itinerary is open-ended, too. This type of cruise frequently extends into multi-year, world-wide voyages. Only age or health concerns brings them back to shore and then frequently not to where they started. Their cruising home has become their actual home, and returning to shore is not based on business or family concerns. Eric and Susan Hiscock and Lin and Larry Pardey are examples of this type of cruiser.

Far more cruisers make a cruising commitment for a certain period of time based on finances, family concerns, kids' education, and employment considerations. Most of these cruises fall into the 1- to 3-year category. More and more people seem able to accommodate this more modest cruising dream without total disruption of their previous lifestyles. When their cruise is over, they generally return to a home base somewhere in the States and reenter the workforce.

Because of advances in communications, the time is almost here when some cruisers (in certain occupations) can actually stay employed while underway. Many have found the cruising experience to be highly gratifying and enriching in their personal and professional lives. The stresses of modern life are somehow put in different perspective following a sabbatical cruise.

If young children are involved, the problems of schooling can be solved with correspondence courses. Cruising kids are frequently ahead of their peers in both subject matter and maturity when they return to school or college.

How Much Does It Cost?

Many of the most frequently asked questions relate to the costs of cruising. If you ask fellow cruisers how much it costs, you get many different answers. Do you count just living expenses or do you include total underway costs which takes into account boat expenses and equipment maintenance? Generally, the questioner wants to know total expenses. That's a more difficult answer, because so much of it relates to intangibles and to the cruisers' lifestyle. How long was their cruise? Was it long enough to require major maintenance expenses such as replacement of sails and canvas, engine overhaul, or electronics updates? Was the boat insured? Did they have unusual medical expenses? How often did they haul out? Did they do their own work? Did their boat require extensive repairs like a blister job? Did they take long inland trips while visiting other countries? Did they frequently return to the States for business, medical reasons, or to visit grandkids? Where did they cruise? Did they eat like the locals when visiting other countries, or insist on "American" food on board and ashore? Did they provision in local markets whenever possible?

It may be possible to generalize somewhat about cruising expenses, but from the above you can see the problem. The answers I received from fellow cruisers about the costs of cruising range from "as much as you've got" to "about $600 a month." If you limit your cruise to between one and three years, which limits major replacement costs, then a conservative "barn door" figure might be $800 to $1200 per month. When cruising on a powerboat, increased fuel costs would raise these estimates significantly, depending on your cruising style and itinerary. Of course you can spend much more (and many do), but you can probably do it for less. Cruising, after you get your boat, can be done quite reasonably and certainly costs less than staying at home—no auto expenses, no business suits, no mortgage, reduced marina costs, cheap food and shelter, and limited taxes and insurance expenses. Cruising need not be just a rich man's avocation. Underway costs can be modified to fit all budgets. You will most likely experience a dramatic drop in living expenses once you cast off your U.S. mooring lines.

Low-budget Cruising

So you've got the urge, but not the bucks! Well, if you're a do-it-yourselfer (male or female) and have determination, you could be out there living your cruising dream sooner than you might think. There are numbers of older, stout, and inexpensive boats that will take you just about anywhere you might want to go. And there are even good smaller boats that are outboard-powered and thus usually less expensive. If you can do the restoration, preparation, and maintenance yourself, you could join many others who have preceded you "down to the sea in ships." Most of the early cruisers were persons like yourself. All they had was a small boat (some engineless), which they built or rebuilt themselves, and little else. Young or old, they accomplished their personal dreams with minimal financial resources. Joshua Slocum, Harry Pigeon, Peter Tangvald, John Guzwell, Bernard Moitessier, and Robin Lee Graham are a very small sampling of highly successful low-budget cruisers. Recently, a rebuilt and highly-reinforced Cal 25 made for California coastal cruising completed a circumnavigation. The skipper and his young wife had two children en route!

Cruising With Kids

Cruising with your kids will create shared family experiences that are hard to duplicate on shore. More and more, our hectic lifestyles seem to individualize experiences that formerly would have been shared within the family. The lives of family members are more and more self-contained: longer business hours, both husband and wife working, more TV, more alone-time for kids, many more activities outside the family, and less time together as a family unit.

For better or worse, cruising instantly throws kids and parents together for extended periods. There are few escapes. This is not to suggest that each family member can't have his or her own personal space where they can spend necessary private time. But on a cruising boat, you must learn to share, get along, and help each other as was never required ashore. Kids learn to take responsibility for sailing and maintaining the boat. When they are old enough, they can stand watches and help in the galley and on topside, too. They learn to row, use the outboard, snorkel and dive, sail, steer, operate the ship's electronics and radios, and even navigate. They learn to read and converse. They see mom and dad working together toward common family goals as they never did at home.

You see kids of all ages cruising. Comments from cruising families suggest that the best time to cruise with your children is before they reach their late teens. Many cruising parents seem to think that for their kids, those late teen years are best spent ashore with their peers. Their decisions are generally based on the need for social development and for advanced schooling.

During the cruise, parental instruction, natural phenomena, differing cultures, and the ship's educational resources (books, tapes, videos, etc.) will be the basis for the intellectual development of children aboard. On cruises longer than one year, you should formalize onboard instruction by enrollment in correspondence courses (K through 8th grade) for each child. The Calvert School (Baltimore, MD 410-243-6030) has had great success providing this type of instruction. In all cases, though, there must be consistent involvement by the parents.

Many times cruising kids place at or above their grade level when they return to formal schooling. They are better readers and conversationalists, and frequently they are more mature than non-cruisers. Cruising is a very positive experience for kids and does not have to be delayed because of their educational needs.

Charter Cruising

Don't forget about charter cruising: those memorable 1- and 2-week trips to exotic places like Greece or Tahiti sailed in new boats prepared and provisioned by the charter company. This is a great way to check out new boats and equipment or to see some beautiful cruising locales that you might want to revisit later on your own boat. It's also an opportunity for the skipper, first mate, or crew members to temporarily escape their hectic lifestyles and test the cruising waters—without the total commitment that a lengthy cruise in their own boat would entail. It's a chance to decide if this is really for you and to avoid the sometimes sad predicament that disillusioned cruisers find themselves in after committing vast amounts of time and money to a lifestyle they didn't fully understand.

The charter experience is an idealized and painless way to prepare yourself. At the same time, it is an opportunity to indoctrinate a reluctant crew member into the pleasures of sailing some of the world's best cruising grounds. And if you don't wish to sail monohulls, there are multihulls and powerboats in many of those charter fleets as well.

Age and Health Concerns

Age does not have to be an important factor in the decision to go cruising. Numbers of senior citizens (both men and women, singles and couples) are out there living their cruising dreams. They compensate in various ways for shortcomings in youthful brawn and agility. Boats sailed by crews in their sixties and seventies are common. If the senior is healthy and active, there is no reason to stay at home.

More important is your general health—and this goes for sailors of all ages. Personal health problems are an important factor in whether a cruise succeeds or not. On-going medical conditions are more commonly responsible for aborted cruises than are boating accidents. You need to have good control of any chronic disorders and have the medication to treat them on board. Your cruising skills, be they brawn or brain, may be critically needed should you become ill. My comments should not imply that there isn't expert medical attention available in many third world countries. Frequently there is, and often the doctors are U.S. trained, especially in Central and South America. But access to medical care and particularly emergency treatment is not as universal as in the States. You and your crew must be ready to administer emergency aid until professional help is available.

Chapter 2

Preparing Yourself For Cruising

(2 to 10 years before departure)

Self-preparation

This area requires the most commitment on your part. Long before your dreamed of departure, perhaps even before you have a boat, you can and should begin your cruising education. There's a lot to learn. Your cruising education can be in several forms, but will probably include course work, personal study, seminars, presentations by other cruisers, and as much practical boating experience as you can squeeze in. It should include work in the following areas: sailing and seamanship; navigation and communications; meteorology; medicine at sea; and vessel maintenance. If your cruise involves others, it may be possible for them to assume vital roles in this intense but highly enjoyable preparation procedure. In the process, the pre-cruise period may be shortened considerably.

Sailing Skills and Seamanship

Do as much sailing as you can. Do it on all kinds of boats and in all kinds of weather. Do it in your own boat or crew for others. Race when you can. Cruisers can learn much from competitive sailors about sail trim, boat speed, sail handling, and maneuvering under sail. Sailing and handling your boat well means getting the most out of your vessel; it is a safety factor that each skipper needs to explore on his or her own boat. Learn the full potential of your boat in all sea and wind conditions, not just on those great sailing days. Learn how to drive her hard when needed and how to reef down to stay dry and comfortable—which is most of the time. Learn what sails and sail combinations are needed to make your boat perform in various conditions. Learn how to hove-to and how to make your boat comfortable in a seaway. Encourage your cruising partners to share these experiences too. The more skilled sailors there are on board, the easier it will be for you, and the less fear and trepidation there will be on deck. Remember, too, the skipper's expertise and leadership in these areas will do much to allay the anxiety of less experienced crew members when it really counts.

Maneuvering Under Power

Under power, a sailboat or single-screw powerboat is frequently awkward to maneuver in tight situations. Windage, prop rotation, and thrust are factors that must be learned and allowed for on every boat—in both forward and reverse. Some boats behave nicely and steer easily in reverse. But some boats defy even the best skippers, seemingly intent on creating confusion and embarrassment for the slightest oversight. Practice stopping in both forward and reverse. Practice docking both port and starboard side. Practice backing into slips. Practice forward docking. Practice turning in the smallest circles, using forward-reverse-forward techniques. Learn which way to turn for the smallest turning radius, because left- and right-hand-propped boats will behave differently. Practice using spring lines to enter and exit awkward docking locations. Practice picking up a mooring can. Learn how to allow for windage and current. While you're at it, learn how to tie up your boat in a seamanlike manner at a fuel dock or berth. (See this chapter, **Marlinespike Seamanship.**) Encourage your mate to gain this expertise and confidence, too. Include your crew members whenever possible. Develop the teamwork that is so obvious on well-handled cruising boats.

Motorsailing

Motorsailing is a tactic commonly used by cruising sailors. But far too many sailors become addicted to their auxiliary engines. Not only is it considered bad form to use your engine on a day when the wind is fair, but it builds engine hours and ultimately creates more engine maintenance for you to perform. Overuse of the auxiliary generally marks the skipper as less than fully seasoned in the eyes of experienced cruisers, not to mention the negative environmental impact and the difficulty you may have in refilling your diesel tanks in some remote locations. In a favorable wind and under full sail, you might actually get there faster under sail alone. This is not to imply that I think you must become a sailing-only purest. You will not find my boat drifting with slatting sails in a dying 3-knot breeze two miles from a quiet anchorage—not when I have a perfectly good auxiliary. After all, that's what it's for!

You should learn to be a good motor-sailor. Learn how to maximize your boat speed when you have to make a landfall or enter an anchorage before dark. Learn how to combine sail and power most efficiently. What sail or sails, with added auxiliary power, will produce the best combination of speed and stability with minimum fuel consumption—your ultimate goal. Learn how to motorsail to windward in a seaway when you just have to get there.

Much of your motorsailing will be with full or partially reefed main, mizzen, or staysail. Your aim generally is to stabilize the boat in the seaway and to make good a course and speed you could not achieve without power assistance. Your course in this situation is probably in preparation for a landfall. Conversely, if you are well at sea in reasonable conditions, you would most certainly want to hoist a jib and fall off to a comfortable course you could maintain under sail alone.

You may have determined you need to make good four, five, or six knots of speed to achieve your next leg in a timely manner or make a landfall before dark. The addition of auxiliary power may be both seamanlike and expedient—whether for safety, weather, or other conditions.

Makes navigation easy -- but don't be lulled into careless practice.

Navigation

The modern navigator has much to be thankful for: no more chronometers, no tables, no sextants. It's almost too simple. The traditionalist will strongly recommend you take the time to master the "discipline" of celestial navigation. But realistically, few do. As a former navigation instructor and co-author of a celestial text, I am saddened to see the end of this nautical art form. It is still true that the prospective cruiser is well advised to take along a celestial calculator (like the Celesticomp V or Merlin II which does all the math and takes the place of those bulky tables and almanacs) and at least a plastic sextant, just in case. But many cruisers are backing up their navigation systems with a second or third GPS instead. (Celestaire at 800-727-9785 has large selection of traditional navigation equipment.)

Modern electronics have done much to simplify the navigator's life. It seems almost sacrilegious to say this, but celestial navigation can and frequently does become just an option for modern skippers. Realistically, there are fewer and fewer traditional navigators out there. They increasingly rely on multiple GPSs and all things electronic (radars, sounders, sonars, auto pilots—sometimes all interfaced) to determine their vessel's position, course, and speed.

But the demands of the sea have not changed. The need for careful navigation, proper plotting procedures, and adequate watch-keeping have not changed. Attention to these details can save your boat and perhaps your life. Modern electronics should not lull you into disregarding basic safety procedures. At the very least, the skipper should be fully trained in the navigation techniques of reading charts, taking bearings, plotting positions, and keeping accurate log entries. Don't let the simplicity of pushing black buttons lull you into careless navigation practices.

Trouble in paradise -- cutter aground.

In the navigation classes I used to teach, I frequently found women to be excellent navigation students. They seem by nature to be neater, more detailed and precise in plotting procedures and navigation techniques. A vessel is well served if more than one person on board can navigate. Two heads are frequently better than one. Over-dependence on one person is dangerous for all. Spread the responsibilities around for the safety of the boat as well as for the interest and satisfaction of the crew.

Communications

Women often excel here, too. Radios and women seem to attract one another. Ladies' natural communication inclinations find a perfect outlet when operating the ship's radios. Radios provide an opportunity to network with others in the cruising fraternity, and to stay in touch with family at home. For the cruiser in distant waters, VHF (very high frequency), SSB (single sideband), and amateur (also called "ham") radios can be the marine equivalents of radios, TVs, and cellular phones at home. Radios are vital for your safety, well being, and morale. Each type radio can provide communication, weather broadcasts, emergency contacts, and informative marine nets for the cruiser. And in an emergency, each radio can broadcast distress calls on its own prescribed frequencies. Remember though, the VHF radio is limited to short-range line-of-sight communication.

Licensing procedures are quite different for each radio. (See Chapter 10, ***Contact Information*** for radio courses by Gordon West.) Earning an amateur or ham radio license requires time and effort, though I have never found a licensed ham who was resentful of the study required to earn his or her "ticket." Because ham licensing is more time-consuming it should not be left to the last minute. Many boats are equipped with all three radios, because each has its special advantages. Some of the newest SSB radios combine both high seas and ham capabilities in one unit. For more information on communications, see ***Weather*** below and Chapter 5, ***Departure Countdown*— Staying in Touch.**

Weather

While underway, a significant amount of your time and effort will be devoted to gathering weather information. What seems so commonplace ashore becomes difficult and demanding when cruising. Most local TV news broadcasts, as well as the Weather Channel on cable TV, provide almost limitless amounts of weather information. They show satellite images, gather gobs of surface information for the whole country, and forecast their predictions days in advance. Other specific marine-weather broadcasts are available via VHF WX channels—when we are concerned enough to listen.

But when we're underway, these will all too soon become unavailable and just distant memories. Once well offshore, you will find no TV, no VHF (except ship-to-ship), and shortly thereafter no AM radio either, because these are all basically line-of-sight communications. Such unappreciated luxuries just are not designed to follow you on your distant wanderings.

Your weather information will come from high-seas broadcasts and images captured on your computer via marine SSB, ham radio, or from a dedicated weather fax (WXfax) receiver. World news will come from British Broadcasting Corporation (BBC) or Voice of America (VOA) broadcasts. Your ship's weather forecaster will have to bunk on board. Probably for the first time, you will have to forecast your local weather based on the ship's instruments and on weather information you've gathered from weather nets on VHF (U.S. water only) or SSB/ham radio (international waters). You will be responsible for collecting the information, interpreting the data, and forecasting the upcoming weather!

What all this leads to is: someone in your crew must prepare for this second most important job on board. This could be a self-study program (Many good weather books are available for the boater.) or, if you're fortunate enough to find one, a good weather-at-sea class offered specifically for yachties. Much like the case with amateur radio licensing, it's a mistake to put this off too long. It takes time to absorb, practice, and digest this material.

Recent advances in satellite communications make it possible to subscribe to private weather information services aboard your boat wherever you cruise. With this link you can also send e-mail, faxes, and distress messages. This service is used by commercial shipping and by some offshore racers. It is expensive. But if your cruising budget allows, it is a very nice way to go. Besides the WX service subscription costs, you will also have to install special onboard communication electronics that allow you to connect to a shore-based relay station through the satellite. Comsat Mobile Communications (800-685-7898) C-Link service utilizes an Inmarsat-C satellite and a marine transceiver like the one manufactured by Trimble Navigation (800-827-8000, ext. 8121) and others. Trimble's small onboard unit is called the Galaxy Inmarsat-C/GPS transceiver. It costs in the neighborhood of $4000. Other less expensive systems utilize radio frequencies to supply proprietary weather information. These high frequency (HF) services also allow for e-mail and fax, but not without charges. (See Chapter 5, ***Departure Countdown*—Staying In Touch.)**

Physical Conditioning

Take time to get yourself in good physical condition and require this of the crew as well. Getting in shape is one of the most important things you can do for your own enjoyment of cruising. Cruising can test you physically, as well as provide time for the complete rest and relaxation that may be part of your cruising goals. Too often the crew and skipper depart on their long-planned dream cruise while they're still in flabby condition from sedentary lifestyles, exhausted from the long and continuous preparations, and anxious to be underway. They think they'll have a chance to rest as soon as they get going and away from departure hassles. But chances are there is still much work to do aboard. Below deck, there will be the final stowing of clothes, gear, and provisions—and now there are all those boat systems to monitor, sails to tend, and watches to stand. Exhaustion and stress are not good conditions for starting your cruising odyssey. Conceivably, the first passage—long before reaching your first idyllic anchorage—could make or break the voyage.

If you are unfortunate enough to encounter some bad weather immediately after departure, you may have a much shorter cruise than expected. Let's hope you and your crew took a serious preparatory shakedown trip before departure. A prudent skipper might decide immediately after departure to find a nearby anchorage, drop the hook, and allow time for all crew members to familiarize themselves with the boat, finish stowing their gear, and get a good rest before continuing.

This can not be a "Love Boat" cruise for anyone. It must be a working voyage for everyone aboard. Take "guests" at your own risk. Both stamina and strength are sometimes needed to safely sail the boat. More than a few cruises are ruined during the first encounter with a squall or bad weather. It can be very frightening to have equipment failures, realize you're overpowered and out of control, and barely have the physical resources to make things right.

Don't forget to have several seasickness remedies on board for the very first leg. This malady, now almost 100% controllable, will most certainly have a very negative impact on the crew. While passagemaking, everyone must be able to lend a hand when called upon. Have non-boating friends join you *after* you are safely at your destination—rather than have them aboard during your passages.

Anchoring

Like your sailing and seamanship skills, anchoring your vessel is something that must be practiced repeatedly if you are to feel comfortable and secure while cruising. If your night's anchorage is to be a place of rest and relaxation, your anchoring technique must be refined enough to avoid those 2 a.m. anchor drills. It takes practice and experience to become good at anchoring. Each new anchorage and changing weather condition will have an impact on your developing anchoring expertise. This is the one area where many new cruisers (and old ones too!) have problems.

In many U.S. boating areas, "having to anchor" can easily be avoided. Docks, marinas, and moorings are convenient and seemingly always available. Such is not the case while cruising. Most of your time will be spent swinging on your own hook. Even when a marina is available, you may come to choose "being at anchor" as your preferred mode for visiting new areas—saving time, money, and docking hassles in the process. You can read all the books about anchoring, but ultimately it is up to you. Actual practice makes perfect (well almost), because anchoring is as much art as science. Developing your skills will help you avoid many a sleepless night, and perhaps save your boat as well. See the Chapter 8, ***Reference Section*—Anchoring and Ground Tackle** for anchoring techniques and ground tackle suggestions.

Medical Preparations

Once you're underway, you may have to provide the medical skills and medications for the welfare of the crew. We can't all instantly become doctors and dentists, but what we can do is thoughtfully prepare prior to leaving for possible medical emergencies and contingencies. That will require assembling a cruising medical kit, learning CPR techniques, and assigning someone in the crew to be the ships "doctor." That person should attend a *Medicine At Sea* type course where emergency procedures, injection skills, and recommended medicines and drugs are discussed, taught, and demonstrated. Properly prepared small craft can become remarkably self-sufficient for all but the most serious cruising emergencies. Via modern communications, the most remote cruising boat can now be connected to professional medical advice.

Medicine At Sea and *Safety At Sea* seminars are often offered near major boating centers of the U.S. If you can't find one, then meet with your family doctor in a private session to learn the basics of suturing and injections, and to familiarize yourself with the drugs and medicines needed for your cruising medical kit. You can also try calling *Cruising World* Magazine; they annually co-sponsor several *Safety At Sea* seminars which often include medical presentations. A list of suggested onboard medicines and supplies for the cruising sailor will be found in Chapter 8, ***Reference Section*—Acquiring Drugs, Medicines, and Supplies.**

Language Skills

If you were fortunate enough to have studied a foreign language in high school or college, it may come in handy now. Spanish and French are the most useful cruising languages. Your first foreign landfalls will most likely be in countries where one or the other is spoken. But don't despair if you aren't fluent or even close for that matter. As your cruising lifestyle slows down, you will have time to study your language books and tapes, and practice on the locals to develop basic and necessary speaking skills. Conversational phrases and numbers will be the most valuable at first. Native speakers may smile and laugh, but they will appreciate your attempts at speaking their language.

We found native speakers to be genuinely helpful whenever we made a sincere effort to communicate. But don't be like some American cruisers who think a second language is just speaking English louder. Take along a good taped language course, and practice underway on each other. Take tourist phrase books, dictionaries, and flash cards—and practice, practice, practice. You may surprise yourself! Your enjoyment of foreign countries and peoples will be vastly increased if you will make the effort to learn even the basic conversational phrases and numbers.

In many ways the pleasures of visiting other cultures, the ability to travel around the country, and the capacity to buy provisions and spare parts—all relate directly to your language skills. Many cruisers take the opportunity to enroll in language schools while abroad. Several Central and South American countries have developed large cottage industries catering to foreign tourists who want individual or small-group instruction in Spanish. Both San Jose, Costa Rica and Antigua, Guatemala are famous for their excellent courses in conversational Spanish for tourists. In some cases, you can actually live with native families while you are studying their language, thus gaining a more complete immersion into the culture. Language study is available in many places. Just inquire when you arrive.

Marlinspike Seamanship - Knots, Bends, Hitches, and Splices

In the old days of iron men and great sailing ships, marlinspike seamanship was practiced and used aboard ship night and day. Knotting and splicing skills could save a man's ship—and also his life. On the off-watch hours, work with knife and marlinespike could lift his spirits with traditional artistry on tusk, bone, wood, and line. Marlinspike seamanship could quickly belay an anchor or beautifully adorn a sailor's sea chest or duffel. Unfortunately, much like celestial navigation, it has been largely lost to the modern voyager. However, the need to properly handle lines, knots and splices has not changed, nor have the sea's demands—they are constant. For the cruising sailor today, mastering about eight knots, a few hitches, and simple splicing techniques is all that's necessary when combined with underway inspections and onboard vigilance. An experienced mariner can usually assess the skill and experience level of other cruisers, merely by observing their knots and splices.

If prospective cruisers will learn how to tie just a few knots, bends, and hitches and know when and how to use them, they will go a long way to ensure the safety and security of the boat and crew.

Below is a list of a few essential knots. There are hundreds and hundreds of others not even counting the decorative uses of line. If you master just these few, you can easily handle the demands of cruising on a small boat. (Incidentally, a *knot* is tied in a line; a *bend* ties two lines together; a *hitch* is tied to an object other than another line.)

Figure-eight Knot

Used as a stopper knot on the end of a sheet or halyard to keep it from running through blocks and sheaves.

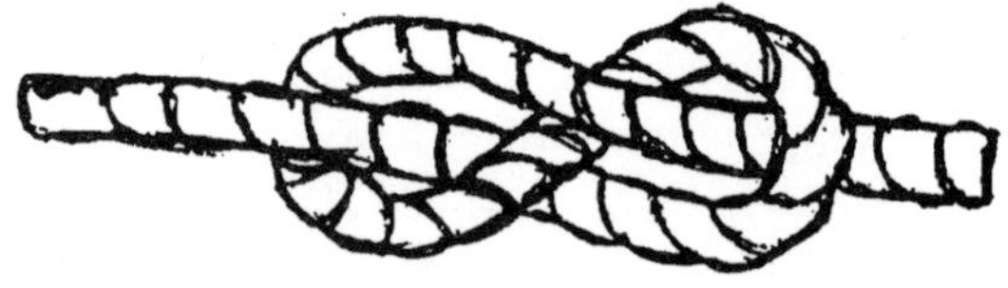

Square or Reef Knot

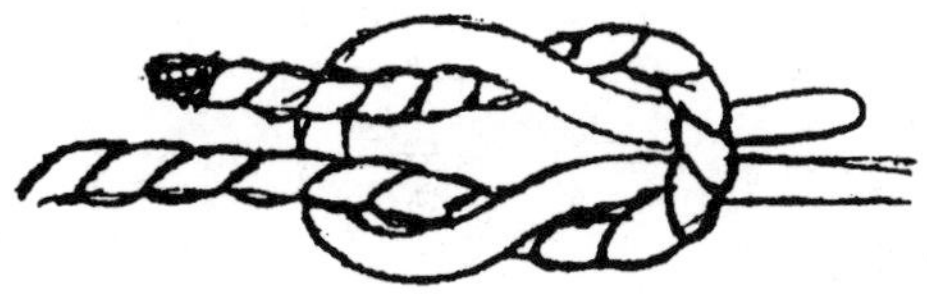

Used to tie two light lines together. Square knots can slip and are difficult to untie. A slipped reef knot (like a half-tied shoe lace) is the best knot for tying reefs in your sail. It will untie with just a single pull, yet hold securely while needed. If you use the regular square knot, you won't be able to untie it under strain.

Bowline (knot)

Used to make a secure eye or loop in a line. Probably the most frequently used knot. Can't be untied under load.

Round Turn and Two Half Hitches

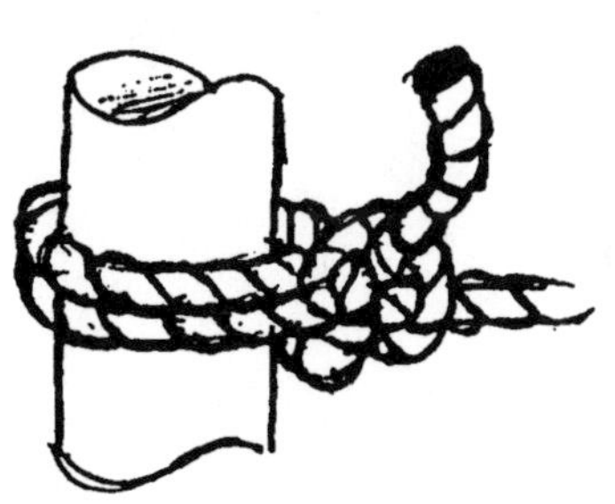

Best hitch for securing your dinghy or your boat. Has many other onboard uses. Easy to untie under load.

Sheet Bend (Single)

Used to tie two lines together. Much preferred to a square knot or interlocking bowlines for this purpose. (Use the double sheet bend for even more security.)

Rolling Hitch

A most useful knot for attaching a line to slippery or round objects. Also used to tie flags on halyards and to tie to another line. When going aloft, use it to secure a safety line to the mast. Must pull downward.

Constrictor Knot

Used as a temporary whipping on line; very helpful when splicing.

Trucker's Hitch

Makes a temporary unslipping loop in the middle of a line to gain a 2:1 purchase. Doesn't sound very nautical, but a trucker's hitch is most useful when you need added purchase to secure something, like your dinghy on deck, etc.

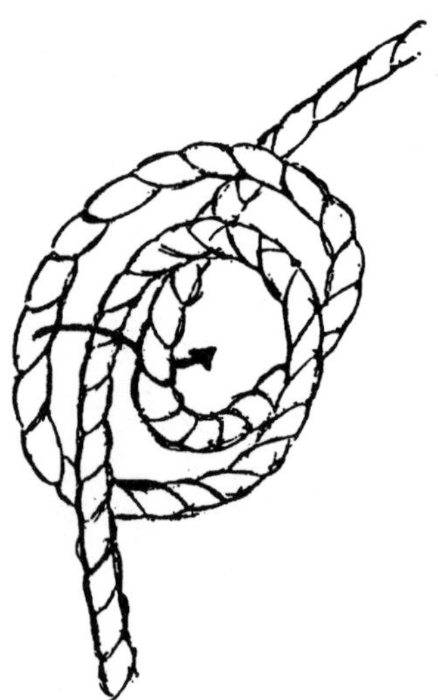

Sea Gasket

Not really a knot, but a very handy way to make up (coil) long lines and anchor rodes. Keeps lines neat and tangle-free.

Another marlinspike skill you will find useful is a nice *whipping* on the ends of your lines. Although a constrictor knot, a plastic tool-dip product, or a hot knife can temporarily keep your line for fraying, only a good whipping done with palm and needle can keep your lines really ship-shape. I've used *Plasti Dip* (used for dipping tool handles, etc.) for fast jobs with surprisingly good results. They make a variation called *Rubber Wrap* that comes in a 4-ounce can with applicator brush. It's very handy for temporarily whipping lines and for coating anything sharp, like cotter pins and bolt heads, that could tear your sails and hands. It comes in several colors. (At hardware stores or from PDI Inc., Circle Pines, MN, 612-785-2156)

In addition to these eight knots, you should develop skill in splicing 3-strand, and braided line. Add a *short splice* (with 3-strand) and an *eye splice* (3-strand and braid) to your marlinspike expertise. These are easy and fun techniques—especially the 3-strand which is easiest. Three-strand splicing technique will let you maintain and repair your anchor rode even if you should find chafe in the middle of the line.

Finally, learn how to properly secure your boat to a cleat. Use the round turn and figure-eight method. But those lines must be laid down correctly on the cleat to pass inspection.

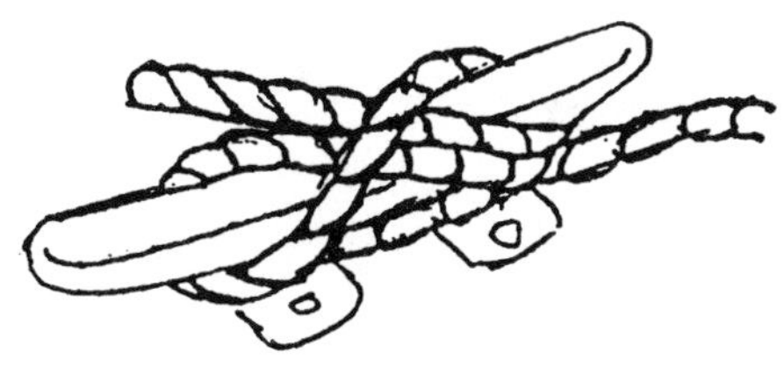

Maintenance Skills

To be self-sufficient when cruising, it is important that you take personal responsibility for maintaining your vessel. There may be no one else available to service your equipment and make necessary repairs. Before departure, actively participate in boat maintenance projects to learn techniques, materials, and products. Watch the professional boat workers do their jobs whenever you can. Visit the sail loft and the rigger's shop. Hang around the shipyard once in a while—even when your own boat is not hauled out. It is surprising how much you can learn just by watching and asking questions of those who maintain boats professionally. When underway, maintenance manuals and schematics are essential if you or a fellow cruiser or a foreign tradesman are to tackle repairs to your complex onboard equipment.

Take the time to acquire service materials and manuals on each piece of your boat's equipment. Make sure you have any necessary and special tools to maintain that equipment. Some machinery requires specialized tools to make repairs—so if you don't have that special tool or gizmo, it won't get fixed.

Before your departure, inquire from dealers, servicemen, and other cruisers what spares and replacement parts to take with you. Most manufacturers and suppliers of marine equipment can furnish recommended spare-parts lists to a cruiser planning a voyage. Once you're underway, needed parts will be difficult or impossible to find except from other cruisers. If the needed repairs require parts or tools you don't have, you could spend days, weeks, or worse waiting for FedEx to bring them to a large city near you. Then you'll have to wait for the local customs people to tax and clear them. Sometimes the "yacht in transit" label on packages and invoices sent to you will keep you from having to pay import duties and local taxes—but not always.

I found the problem with the head -- an eel in the intake valve.

Involving Other Crew Members

As you can see from all of the above, there is much to do in preparation for a cruise. It can be much easier if these responsibilities are shared with your sailing partner or other members of the crew. It turns them into participants rather than spectators, and in the process involves them in the excitement of preparing for their upcoming cruising adventure. And it's much more fun to play in the game than just warm the bench.

Chapter 3

Finding Your Dream Boat

(2 to 5 years before departure)

If you haven't already found your cruising home, one of the most important, most pleasurable, and most trying experiences still awaits you in your search for the perfect cruising boat. Whether you can afford to buy a new boat from a top builder, or your finances require that you look for used boat bargains, the vessel you select will become your floating home for as long as you cruise. Its strong points will bring you repeated pleasure and any shortcomings will be continually evident—and will constantly annoy.

There are many used boats out there that are almost better than new. Someone else shook-them-down to find the builder's bugs. Someone else equipped the boat for cruising—a major job in itself. Someone else spent countless hours and dollars bringing the stock boat up to cruising trim. But, concerning pre-owned boats, the reverse can also be true. Old gear and equipment (especially electronics) can all too quickly become outdated and unusable. Previous abuse or hard use can make an otherwise fine design unsuitable for your needs.

Talk with yacht surveyors, check with brokers, subscribe to boating magazines, watch ads in papers and sailing magazines, attend boat shows, walk the docks, and talk to owners of similar boats. If you would like to contact other owners of a particular boat you are considering, *Cruising World* magazine (900-988-2275) in their "*Another Opinion*" column allows you to do just that for a $5 service fee. They will fax a list of owners who are willing to discuss the merits of their own boats. *Practical Sailor* magazine (fax/203-661-4802) has comprehensive evaluations on over 80 boats, which they will fax to you at $4.50 per page (average report is four pages long). You need to fax them your name, address, and credit card number with expiration date, and identify the boat you're interested in.

The boat you select will significantly affect your enjoyment of cruising. Take your time, ask millions of questions, and sail, sail, sail. Sail as many different boats as you can. Sail with friends, rent with sailing clubs, charter cruise, and crew for others. It is dangerous to buy a boat without lots of first hand, on-the-water experience.

If you're looking for a cruising powerboat, your efforts should be similar: to get at-sea experience aboard many different boats before trying to reach a decision on your personal offshore cruiser. The selection process can take many months, but your time and energy will be well spent. If you want to test powerboats in exotic locations, you can now charter in many world-wide locations and have a great vacation too. See the back of boating magazines for charterboat companies that feature powerboats in their fleets.

Vessel Selection—Cruising Rigs

Choosing a boat for cruising is almost as tough as picking a mate. If you've been boating for a while, you probably have already developed strong likes and dislikes about cruising boats and don't need people pushing their personal preferences on you. What you may want to know, though, is what is currently "out there" and then list some things to consider if you haven't yet made up your mind. If you've got your cruising boat already, go on to the next section.

By far the largest number of cruising boats are sailboats. In the Caribbean, Mexico, and the Med, there are small but growing numbers of cruising powerboats. Not many small powerboats cross oceans, but even these numbers are increasing. Of the sailboats out cruising, most are single-mast rigs—sloops and cutters. Next come multihulls (of all rigs) and ketches. Yawls, schooners, and cat boats bring up the rear. My best guess is that 75% to 80% of cruising sailboats are sloops or cutters. That percentage is probably not much different from that found in most U.S. marinas. Talk with any experienced sailor and he or she will probably have a personal preference with regards to rigs. If you confine your search for a cruising boat to sloops, cutters, and ketches, you will probably not go too wrong.

Powerboat shoppers should limit their search to semi- or full-displacement hulls. High-speed, multi-engine, and high horsepower boats will not provide the fuel economy and long range required for extended cruising.

Purchase Considerations

Here is a list of things that you should check, consider, and approve prior to any purchase.

Pre-purchase Survey

Begin your search for the "perfect boat" with a checklist of things you have determined essential for your new cruising home. List those things you consider important for a cruising boat to have. Include things like rig, interior layout, engine horsepower, hull material, underwater shape, sail inventory, standard equipment, special cruising gear, etc. You can call this your *purchase survey* and it will save lots of time. It will allow you to eliminate many boats, both new and used, that do not fit your criteria. As you inspect different vessels, you will start to develop strong opinions about various design concepts, interior layouts, and equipment selections. At this point you can begin modifying your *purchase survey* to reflect your developing nautical tastes.

The *purchase survey* can now also include a list of special cruising gear. This is equipment that you hope to have on your boat when you're ready to start cruising. Will you need a watermaker, a wind vane, solar panels, EPIRB, SSB radio, autopilot, liferaft, and more ground tackle? The list can go on and on. If the boat has not been previously cruised, there may be much left to do and lots of cruising equipment you will still need to buy. In your offer, allow for this needed equipment and any necessary repairs or upgrades. If you don't, you could easily exceed your cruising budget and delay your departure. This is where your now refined *purchase survey* can be most helpful. You will already have defined and listed the essential cruising equipment you need. This information should help in structuring your offer. Your decision here will either speed or delay your cruising plans.

Eventually you will find a boat that seems to fit most of your needs, both nautical and financial. If the hull, rig, deck, and interior layout passes your inspection; if the boat is a delight to your eye as she sits in the water; and if the interior, galley and head pass muster, you are probably getting close. If you are seriously interested in this boat, it may be time to make an offer and ask for a sea trial. If you are a serious buyer, many individual sellers would be willing to give you a test sail even before you submit a formal offer. If you are working with a broker, you will need to make a formal offer and put down a deposit before a sea trial can be scheduled.

On some new boat purchases, the buyer can expect to spend an additional 30% to 50% of the purchase price to get the boat cruise-ready. Be careful here, you don't want your cruising dream to "go down with the ship." Don't price yourself out of achieving your cruising goals. ***Go now with what you can afford—you may not get another chance.***

Hull and Underbody—Sail

If the yacht designer has been successful in capturing those qualities that contribute to a safe and seaworthy cruising boat, he has completed his job admirably. If his design is dry in a seaway, stiff in a breeze, sails like a dream, and is rock-solid at anchor, he should be knighted—for that's the kind of cruising boat we're all looking for.

Recent trends in sailing hulls are toward beamier boats with wide transoms and aft boarding ladders. I do not suggest that these are necessarily better or safer than older and more traditional designs, but they do allow room for lots of creature comforts below. As such, modern cruising designs are very appealing to the boatshow shopper. For the prospective boat buyer who wants to cruise beyond the next marina, there are many other fine vessels available, both new and used, that combine the qualities desired by offshore sailors—safety, seaworthiness, and comfort, combined with the ability to make reasonably fast passages.

The vast majority of American production boats are constructed of fiberglass. Other boats are built of steel or aluminum, but in smaller numbers. Metal hulls are best suited for one-off production, so you won't find too many examples. Quite a few European boats are built in metal—some with innovative designs and cruising gear. They can be seen wherever you cruise. Florida is a good stateside location where you can find and inspect such vessels.

The modern cruising boat will probably have some sort of modified underbody. Traditionally, boats were made of wood with full keels, attached rudders, and external ballast. More recently, American cruising yacht development has evolved to feature modified underwater profiles which produced lighter, faster, and more maneuverable vessels. Hull shapes have evolved from full keel, to modified keels, to fin keels with spade rudders. Many modern designs allow for reduction of wetted surface with increased performance and maneuverability. A design that incorporates a skeg-mounted rudder also protects that critical element from underwater damage. Many boats currently cruising have some sort of modified underbody. But there are also many successful examples of both traditional full-keel boats as well as all-out racers currently cruising.

Hull and Underbody—Power

Grand Banks 42

Trawler-type, semi-displacement hulls (such as Grand Banks boats) comprise the majority of non-sail vessels one currently sees on extended coastal cruises. Voyages to Alaska or Newfoundland are well within the range of well-found trawlers. Mexico, the Bahamas, the Caribbean basin, and Central or South America can be added to your itinerary, if you're headed south from either the East or West Coast. Boats with single screws (for increased fuel economy) are best suited for the longer passages (300 to 500 miles) you will sometimes need to make. Cruising powerboats can also be equipped with masts and steadying sails for increased stability.

To cross oceans, you will need the extended cruising range and sea kindliness that only a vessel designed for this type of cruising will provide. Ocean-cruising powerboats are not common. A 46-foot Nordhavn recently completed an east-about circumnavigation. She was built by the same company that produces Mason sailboats—P.A.E. of Dana Point, CA (714-496-4848). The Nordhavn 46 is designed with a long deep keel, carries 8000# ballast, is full-displacement, single screw, and cruises at 8.3 knots. This boat was equipped with a single engine—a 140 HP Lugger (John Deere). She carried 1000 gallons of fuel.

Offshore, a full-displacement hull will provide the most comfortable ride and the best fuel economy. A full keel protecting a large, slow-turning propeller which is positioned directly forward of the rudder can provide steering control in heavy weather or when forced to run directly before the seas.

Rigs

Here is a brief overview of the basic sailing rigs and their qualities as they apply to cruising sailboats:

Sloops

Most popular rig. Single mast. Simple rig. Easy to sail. Often provides room topside to carry dinghies on the foredeck or coach roof. Can be modified and rigged as a cutter for heavy weather. Good to windward. Watch out for lightly constructed production boats designed only for local and inshore sailing.

Cutters

Single mast. Preferred by many long-distance cruisers for offshore work. Allows easy setting of staysails and storm jibs on inner forestay. Boat balances easily with reduced sail. Little room on deck for dinghy. Foredeck often cluttered. Good to windward.

Ketches

Two masts, more rigging. Traditional, older rig. Sails best off the wind. Extra mast can reduce cockpit and interior space. Mizzen mast provides good place to mount awnings and antennas. Two masts allow for extra sails and reduce individual sail size without reducing sail area. A bit more work to sail. Mizzen mast can clutter cockpit area.

Yawls

Two masts, more rigging. Older design. Has small mizzen mast placed well aft. Mizzen mast is smaller than on ketches. Extra rigging clutter and reduced room below decks. Mizzen provides good place to mount awning and shade screens. Allows for use of riding sail while at anchor to steady boat.

Schooners

Two masts. Traditional rig. Powerful, off-wind performer. Uses extra sails and rigging. Most schooners are larger boats—above 50 feet. Foremast shorter that mainmast. Seldom found in cruising fleets. More work to sail than single-mast rigs.

Cat Boats

One unstayed mast. No Jib. No standing rigging. Simplest rig. Large mainsail and long boom. Limited sail flexibility. Little deck room. Most cat boats under 35 feet. Best used for local and coastwise cruising. Easy to sail.

Multihulls

Light, fast, unballasted hulls. Boat sails flat with little heel. Can capsize, but not sink. Good in shoal areas. Many found in tropical cruising areas. Both catamarans and trimarans are quite popular. Large interiors and deck areas. Designed with all types of sailing rigs. Wide beam requires special slips and berths in marinas.

Cruising Powerboats

Generally one engine, displacement or semi-displacement, trawler or ocean cruising-type hulls. Cruising powerboats require economical fuel usage for extended range and large tankage. Owners must be self-sufficient—there are few qualified mechanics or electricians available in remote cruising areas.

Deck

As you walk about the deck of a previously owned boat you're considering buying, notice how firm and solid it feels under foot. For stiffness, many decks are constructed like sandwiches—with fiberglass-wood-fiberglass as the common laminate. If water penetrates this sandwich, it can becomes spongy and soft. Repairs to a water-damaged deck can require extensive and expensive repairs—beware. Another top-side damage that can be easily spotted is hairline cracking that indicates stress points. Look for hairline cracks in cockpit corners and check around the mast step or wherever fittings and equipment are mounted. Inside the boat, check overhead to see if the headliner is discolored or stained. If it is, it could indicate deck leaks from above.

Blisters

Blisters are a problem in some fiberglass hulls. Generally they are not visible or noticeable above the waterline. When your prospective boat is hauled, your surveyor is trained to detect these problems and will certainly note them in his report. In some cases, the problem can be so severe as to destroy an entire hull, but this is quite rare. The causes of blisters are complex and relate to the chemistry of fiberglass resin and water absorption in the hull. Don't buy a boat with severe blistering until these problems are resolved. Repairs to damaged bottoms can be as simple as grinding through the gel coat to repair and fill a few small, superficial blisters. But a major repair job could require stripping the gel coat from the entire hull, drying the hull (weeks or months) to remove accumulated moisture, and then gradually building layers of impermeable epoxies and fillers back to the original hull thickness. This is an expensive repair. But if properly done, it returns the hull to an almost new condition. Thankfully, improved resins in newer boats avoid most of the earlier blistering problems of fiberglass hulls.

Mast and Standing Rigging

If the mast is aluminum, check to see that it is in good condition. Is it raw aluminum, painted, or anodized? Is it free of heavy corrosion where the rigging, sail track, spreaders, and fittings attach? Is the rigging size adequate for that size boat (check similar-sized cruising boats)? Oversized rigging and turnbuckles would be ideal for a cruising boat. Check the base of the mast (on the keel or at the deck) for heavy corrosion or damage. If the mast is wood, it must be surveyed at the base, the masthead, and spreaders for dry rot.

With your magnifying glass, check the turnbuckles and swages for hairline cracks. If any are found, they will need replacement. Inspect the tangs, bolts, and fittings that attach to the mast and spreaders. Most purchase surveys do not include rigging inspection above deck level. The surveyor does not go aloft. It will probably cost extra and you may have to hire a rigger to do it, but ask for this too! If you're going to cruise this boat, you need to know, before purchase, the condition of the rigging all the way to the masthead. Some riggers suggest replacing all standing rigging (shrouds and stays) every 10 years, even if it appears to be all right.

Some modern fiberglass boats step the mast on deck. This has both advantages and disadvantages. A deck-stepped mast avoids the necessity of the mast extending through the middle of your salon below decks. But sometimes, if not properly engineered, a deck-stepped mast may not adequately transfer its load to the keel. This can lead to deck stress and bulkhead failure. Be sure to check the deck near the mast for hairline cracks and signs of flexing. Inspect the load-bearing bulkhead directly below the mast for sign of stress or delamination.

When properly engineered, deck-stepped masts can provide more room below and even save the spar should you have a rigging failure. In the case of a dismasting, the whole rig goes overboard intact. This allows for possible salvage and reuse, and avoids tearing up the deck en route.

Running Rigging and Hardware

Many stock-production boats could easily use one-size-larger sheets, halyards, blocks, and winches for cruising. This provides a redundancy of strength and makes for ease of use by the crew. It's much easier to sheet a jib or haul a halyard with larger diameter lines and bigger winches. If your boat uses ½-inch line, try 5/8-inch; if it's 5/8-inch, go to ¾- inch. Carefully check the blocks and winches on your prospective dream boat. Compare them with actual cruising boats of similar size. Blocks and winches carry tremendous loads in heavy weather. In a cruising boat, it's not just the initially-rated strength of a fitting that must be considered. You must also allow for the effects of constant stress and abuse in a hostile saltwater environment.

If you are fortunate enough to buy a boat with truly adequate self-tailing sheet winches, you will count your blessings many times over whenever the wind picks up. Self-tailers are not quite as important for other uses such as halyards, etc., but on many well-found boats every winch will be a self-tailer. Yes, they are more expensive, but in this case well worth it. It's like having three hands or another crew member available when you really need them. You will not regret your decision to equip your vessel with oversized self-tailing winches. On your sea trial, check to see that each member of the crew can haul in the jib in a good breeze. If not, consider upgrades before your departure and adjust your purchase price to allow for these.

Move carefully along the deck—inspecting every piece of hardware and every block. Is it big enough and strong enough to take constant punishment and abuse? In heavy weather, a broken halyard or block can lead to severe consequences. I had my worst night at sea when a mainsheet traveler block failed in bad weather.

Anchor-handling Equipment

Has the designer or previous owner of the vessel given thought to the demands of constant anchoring when cruising in remote areas? Is there a rugged electric anchor windlass? There are good manual windlasses, too, but electric ones provide a safety factor for tired crews. Are there strong rollers for two bow anchors? Will the anchor(s) remain firmly in place even with heavy seas hitting the bow? Does the boat use all chain or a combination nylon rode and chain? Remember, all chain is preferred in coral waters. Does the windlass pull straight from the

Horizontal anchor system on powerboat.

Vertical windlass and anchor system on a sailboat. Note the spare Danforth anchor.

bow rollers to the windlass without chafe and stow the chain in a chain locker with drainage overboard? Can a second anchor be easily deployed and retrieved from the bow? Is there provision for using a stern anchor to Med-moor or to limit boat-swing in a tight anchorage?

Sailing and Sea-keeping Qualities

A good sailing boat (or sea boat if you're a powerboater) will always be a pleasure for the crew. If it is lively underway, easy to handle and maneuver, and simple and stiff to sail; if it will keep going in winds under 10 knots; if getting the sails and anchor up is a cinch; and if it also performs well under power—then your boating pleasures will be abundant indeed. You don't need lots of high-tech rigging and complicated gear. That's just more stuff for you to maintain and which ultimately may fail or break down. It is surprising how many cruising boats are selected for every reason except their sailing and sea-keeping abilities. This issue should be a no-compromise matter. This is where your growing sailing and boating experience will come in handy—in evaluating your new cruising home.

Cockpits

You'll be spending a lot of time in the cockpit (or pilot house if you're a powerboater). Is it comfortable with adequate back support? Is it big enough to sleep in when in the tropics? Can you totally relax there to read a good book? Is it good for entertaining and those great cruiser get-togethers? Does it have a folding cockpit table? Is it too big for a heavy weather passage when a wave-filled cockpit could be dangerous? Can you easily work the boat from the safety of the cockpit in bad weather? Can a dodger and spray curtains be fitted to provide protection for the crew when underway? Does it provide a couple of cozy crew positions behind the dodger when it's wet, cold, and heavy going? Is there adequate stowage in hatches and lazarette for the endless things you need to stow topside? Can you see and access all necessary switches, instruments, electronics, and engine controls from topside? Is there a big manual bilge pump or emergency bilge pump available from the cockpit? Can you reach a fire extinguisher without going below?

Galleys

The arrangement and location of the galley is a most important consideration for a cruising boat. A Galley should be located amidships in the area of least motion. It should be out of the traffic pattern and provide a secure position for the cook to prepare food without being tossed about in a seaway. On all but the smallest cruising boats, sinks should be double, deep, and located as close as possible to the boat's centerline. This keeps water from splashing out or flooding back and allows for drainage even when heeling. For safe food preparation while underway, "L" and "U" shaped galleys supply additional security by providing enclosed working areas. A galley safety belt should also be available for cooking underway. Wear a special cooking apron and shoes in the galley to avoid accidents—and never cook in your bathing suit.

A willing cook (Anna), deep sinks, bread board, pressure cooker, gimbaled stove, U-shaped galley.

On mid-sized boats above 33 feet or so, the galley should be equipped with a 2- to 4-burner gimbaled stove with oven. It should have a sliding pin to lock it down when you want to keep it stable. And it should burn propane fuel. Propane is internationally available, is inexpensive, and is the fuel of choice for most boaters. Throughout the world it is used it for domestic purposes in the towns and villages you will visit. Other cooking fuels like alcohol, kerosene, or natural gas are difficult to find in remote locations and are often expensive. Although rare, the possibility of propane explosions requires careful galley installations and proper gas connections aboard boats—and cautious usage thereafter. All systems should incorporate solenoid cut-off safety switches and valves. Some boats have vapor detectors for added safety.

Most boats today will have hot and cold pressure water in the galley. But pressure water systems waste lots of water, just like at home. To save your vessel's water supply, add manual pumps to the sinks—at least on the cold-water side. You will rarely need hot water in the tropics, but hot water will still be available from the pressure system if you should need it. Add another manual pump for salt water. In clean anchorages you can use this for all your dish washing. (You'll never taste the salt after drying.) You'll find it can save up to 50% of your fresh water. Some cruisers also use salt water for some of their cooking. By the way, Joy soap works great in salt water—lots of suds. It can also be used for salt water bathing!

Consideration of galley equipment would certainly include the following: good lighting (for night passages, choose fixtures that have both white and red bulbs); a small directional 12-volt fan; good ventilation; a fire extinguisher; and adequate storage for pans, utensils, dishes, cooking supplies, and stores. A pressure cooker with a locking lid will come in handy for cooking in heavy weather, for taking hot food to other boats or ashore, and for shortening cooking times (great for reducing cabin heat in the tropics).

Heads

Much like galleys, heads must be positioned correctly within the boat to avoid losing the service of this most important facility in rough seas. Because of the exaggerated motion, a head placed too far forward or too far aft will become unusable in heavy weather. The perfect head would be installed amidships or slightly aft, would have an enclosed shower (curtained or separate from the toilet and basin area), a toilet that faces fore or aft (easier to use when underway), and a wash basin that drains without flooding back when on a heel. A shower separated from the rest of the head (found mostly on boats above 40 feet) helps to keep the rest of the facility dry and simplifies clean up. If the shower pump pumps the shower pan completely dry, that helps too. The basin should be large enough to really wash your face in, and the counter should include a large mirror with good light—remember, both red (now sometimes blue) and white bulbs are needed for night passagemaking.

Engines and Engine Room

Is the boat adequately powered? Most cruising sailboats need at least one horsepower per foot of boat. Diesel power is the only safe way to go—little chance of fire or explosion. A number of small cruising boats (20 to 28 feet) can be successfully cruised with power supplied by outboard motors. These boats are gasoline powered, of course, but the gas is outside the boat and explosive vapors can't accumulate below.

With powerboats, you'll probably be looking for a single engine/single screw deep- keeled vessel. Only this configuration will give you the range capability and sea kindliness you'll want for extended coastal cruising. You don't need high cruising speed and large horsepower—it's economical fuel usage, large fuel tanks, and long-range capabilities that make cruising possible for powerboats. If you're buying a previously owned boat, get a thorough check-out on all mechanical systems. You don't have a secondary propulsion system, as a sailboat does. The engine must be diesel powered and completely reliable.

In any case, can the engine be serviced by you? Is it properly vented and exhausted to supply adequate air flow to the engine room, even in the tropics? Does it have a built-in fire-protection system? Is there a permanent engine room light installed for servicing and maintaining engine-room equipment? Is there adequate room to change oil, change filters, tighten the stuffing box, etc.? Some marine-engine installations do not allow adequate access for the frequent service that cruising-boat systems require. If it isn't convenient, you'll find a way to avoid doing it. Marine maintenance for a voyaging vessel is much more intense than maintaining your house and car at home—or your boat in a marina for that matter.

You will be the skipper of a craft that has its own propulsion; generates its own electricity; has its own water system, refrigeration plant, and waste management equipment; and provides its own navigation and communication systems. Poor access to boat equipment leads to poor preventive maintenance and potentially serious problems for the cruising sailor. By the way, be sure to require a thorough engine survey by a qualified diesel mechanic before purchasing any used boat. You can even go so far as to have the engine oil tested to determine if there is excessive wear occurring internally.

Companionway

Many boats have companionway ladders that are awkward or too steep. Since the crew will make countless trips up and down the ladder, it should be comfortable, not too steep, have adequate grab rails, and have non-skid treads. Do you always have to back down or does it allow descent like stairs in a house? Ladders can be dangerous and are a source of potentially serious and incapacitating onboard accidents. Even in the roughest seas when the boat may be on an extreme heel, the ladder must be safely accessible by the crew. If you have reservations about your ladder, check to see if strong grab rails can't be added beside or above the ladder for added security.

Cabin Layout

Every experienced sailor will have personal preferences about the interior cabin layout. If you're just starting to look for your cruising home, consider layouts that will work while underway, not just while entertaining in the marina. Some boats displayed at boat shows look great in marina environments but fail to provide safety and comfort at sea. The interior arrangement you select must provide comfortable sleeping berths (low, amidships) for the off-watch crew while passagemaking, a head that's usable even in heavy weather (fore- or aft-facing heads are best when it's rough), a galley area that is secure and safe in all conditions, adequate storage, and ample ventilation and illumination. For the tropical cruising most of us want to do, ventilation is of the highest priority.

Inspect many different boats. Look also at boats that have been cruised previously, not just the new models at the brokerage. Talk with experienced cruisers to determine what features really are essential and desirable on long cruises—traditional arrangements have prevailed for good reason. Good ventilation, adequate grab rails (even in the head), good lighting, ample stowage and shelving, a useable chart table, a good head (hopefully with separate shower), comfortable berths (sea berths too) will go a long way to keep spirits up, even on difficult passages.

The Sea Trial

After you have found the boat that most closely matches your *purchase survey*—and passes inspection with the first mate—it's time for a sea trial. Give your spouse a veto power here, because his or her approval is important for successful and happy cruising.

By this time, you and the seller have most likely agreed on an acceptable price. Up to this point you have assumed that all systems and equipment will perform satisfactorily. Now it is the time to test that assumption.

The purpose of the sea trial is to check out everything that could not be thoroughly inspected or operated at the dock. If you're new to boating, now would be a good time to ask an experienced cruiser to go with you. Many important details not easily visible to the new boater will be immediately obvious to a more experienced sailor. Try to pick a day with enough wind to really sail the boat and test all equipment underway. It is now or never for this. Otherwise, it may not be until after you've signed the papers that you discover the autopilot doesn't work or the windlass is frozen, etc.

Test the engine thoroughly. Run it at cruising speeds (5 to 8 knots depending on boat size) for 20 to 30 minutes, then check the heat. It should be between 170° F and 190° F for best operation (160° F for salt-water cooled engines). Test all related equipment like transmission and engine instrumentation. Check the electronics and electrical equipment. Sail the boat hard if the wind allows and use different sail combinations. Inspect the condition of all sails, halyards, rigging, and winches. Use the roller furling. Anchor the boat. Use the windlass and inspect anchors, chain, and rode. They must all be free of rust, corrosion, and abrasion, because your ground tackle will be one of the most important systems onboard. Inspect and use every piece of equipment that you will need to rely on when you are cruising.

If you find problems, but you're still interested in the boat, you will need to adjust the purchase price accordingly.

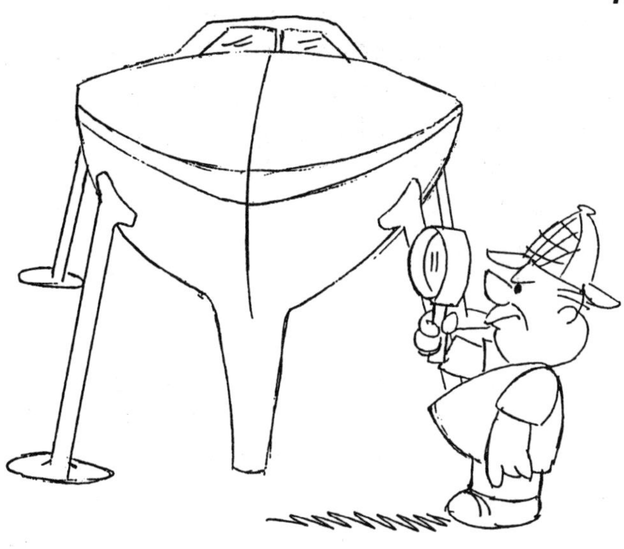

The Marine Survey

After you have found your boat, agreed on a price with the seller, and had the sea trial, the vessel should be hauled out of the water at a shipyard for a marine survey. Unless you're buying a new boat from a broker, you will want a marine survey to ensure the quality and seaworthiness of the vessel. The surveyor will check the integrity of the hull, rig, safety equipment, and related items. He will normally not inspect or operate the engine, will not climb to the top of the mast, will not sail the boat, and will not operate electronic equipment other than to turn it on and off to see if it is functional.

Your purchase agreement and deposit should be contingent upon the vessel passing a satisfactory sea trial, which you will have already completed, and a marine survey. This final inspection of the hull, deck, and equipment is what you're paying the marine surveyor to do. He or she has the professional expertise that protects you from buying a lemon. Depending on the boat size, the surveyor will spend from a few hours to most of a day crawling, probing, poking, tapping, and looking into every space and locker on the boat. He is looking for possible problems, flaws, and deficiencies that would need correction before you could cruise the boat safely.

You should select your surveyor carefully. He will be working on your behalf to make sure you have selected the best boat available for your needs. And he should be selected by you—not the brokerage or the present owner, because their primary interest is to sell the boat. The surveyor's charges are based on the length and size of the boat. When he's finished, he will submit a printed report, perhaps several pages long, describing the condition of the vessel as he perceives it, plus his recommendation for repairs, improvements, and upgrades that he feels are necessary and appropriate. Armed with this information, you can 1) continue with the purchase agreement; 2) renegotiate the price; 3) buy the boat "as is;" or 4) back out of the sale, paying only for the survey costs and haul-out expense.

Do some research to determine which surveyor has the best credentials. Generally each geographic area will have several who have reputations for thoroughness and fairness. Tell him about your cruising plans and get his candid opinions about the suitability of this vessel for the planned usage. Review with him the type of survey you want—a complete out-of-the-water survey, a partial in-the-water survey, or an "insurance survey." Determine what will and will not be surveyed. Does it include rigging aloft? How about an engine survey? This is highly recommended (especially for powerboats), unless you happen to be a diesel mechanic. The more input you have in the process, the better.

Altering a Stock Boat for Cruising

Don't be dismayed if you have found a near-perfect boat, but it seems to have several shortcomings for your needs. If it has the crucial items you have determined to be most important, you may find it easy to correct the other things it needs to become a good cruising boat. Much can be done to improve a vessel for cruising. Interiors can be changed, storage can be increased, tankage can be enlarged, sloops can become cutters, ventilation can be improved, accommodations can be altered—and on and on. Try to make allowance for any planned alterations in your purchase price, so as not to bust the cruising budget.

Arrange to have one or more experienced cruisers from your area do a walk-through cruise survey on your boat to determine what changes, improvements, or additional equipment they would recommended to improve its cruisability. Find boaters with real cruising backgrounds for this informal survey and not just long-time boaters. And be sure to get female input too. Ladies should develop their own lists of improvements. Your sailing partner will offer significant suggestions in this process. Men and women often approach the cruising experience from different points of view—but both are important to successful and happy voyaging.

There are some unique perspectives that come from cruising that are not learned until you are personally exposed to that experience. Don't try to re-invent the wheel here; use the experience and expertise of others to help you with the tough decisions ahead, decisions that will make your cruising life safer, easier, and more fun. Promise some cold beer and sandwiches, and you'll probably find several ex-cruisers who would be willing to help you develop a list of changes, alterations, or upgrades for your boat.

Adding a hardtop dodger.

Your trip "surveyors" will come up with ideas that you could not even imagine until you've been exposed to the cruising life for a while. Do this with more than one person if you can. Try to determine where they are coming from and if their basic idea of cruising is similar to your own. Are they from the "keep it simple, stupid" group, or from the "I'm only going if I can go first class" crowd? Or are they somewhere in between? Determine where you are on this scale, because it will made a big difference in the way you attack the problem of preparing the boat for cruising and in the equipment you will add.

After you have completed several surveys, try to consolidate the recommendations and determine which projects you will tackle. Then get started. Talk with a ship's carpenter, rigger, or electrician to determine what could be done and how much it would cost, if you can't do it yourself. The things you can't easily change are hull shape, rig, engine power, and basic deck layout. The rest is open to modification and possible change.

Chapter 4

Outfitting Your Vessel For Cruising

(1 to 4 years before departure)

Congratulations! If you're reading this section, it means you've probably already made one of cruising's toughest decisions: that of selecting your home afloat. If you are like most other cruisers, you and your crew are already planning alterations, upgrades, and equipment add-ons. Allow ample time for this stage of your preparations. It can take months to select and install all the special cruising gear that you'd like to have on board. In fact, your to-do list will get so long, you will probably leave before you cross off all the items. Almost every person who has cruised has had the same experience. Don't be afraid to commit to a timetable, though. Start the count down! Otherwise you may join the dreamers who are perpetually planning—but who never cast off.

Depending upon your boat, here are a few things to consider and place near the top of your pre-departure list:

Sails

Modern roller-furling systems have done much to simplify sail selection for the average cruising sailor. Many boats now have roller-furling jibs, and an increasing number also have roller-furled mains. Roller-furlers on the jib have been proven to be highly reliable even in the worst of conditions. They keep the crew off the foredeck in bad weather and allow one well designed furling jib to do the work of several hanked-on sails of earlier times. So far, furling mains have not achieved such high marks, although some skippers now rave about them. Good furling gear greatly reduces the need for sail changes while underway. At the same time, it improves safety factors by allowing the crew to reef and adjust the boat's sail area from the safety and convenience of the cockpit.

If you're converting from older hanked-on sails to roller-furling, be sure to work closely with a good cruising sailmaker to recut or modify your old sails to perform in a partially furled manner. In the case of jibs, this will require removing the old sail hanks and adding the "bead" that will actually feed into the furler extrusion. In addition, soft foam sheeting can be sewn into the luff (leading edge) of your sail to remove the excess draft (belly) when the sail is used partially furled. As you furl the sail for heavier weather, the sail must become flatter and flatter for the stronger winds expected. A properly-cut furling jib should allow you to sail at least up to a close reach and still retain sail shape and efficiency.

Many new cruisers spend far too much money on specialized cruising sails designed for every weather eventuality of an extended world cruise. These sails only clutter up the forepeak, reduce the budget, and take valuable storage space that could be used for other things. For mom and pop cruisers planning to sail in moderate latitudes, most heavy-weather sails will never come out of the bag. This is assuming that the boat is equipped with working sails in good condition, and it has a good manual reefing system on the main with roller-furling on the jib. You will find much greater use for a drifter or cruising spinnaker than for the storm trysail. In fact, many cruising sailboats are poorly equipped to sail in the light weather one frequently encounters. If you start with a strong, well made mainsail with two or three rows of reef points (depending on sail size) and a furling jib designed to sail partially furled, you will have most of what you need. Add a storm jib and an asymmetrical cruising chute (needs no pole) for light weather, and you're about there. But talk with people who have actually cruised the areas you want to sail. Ask them what sails they used and what sail-repair problems they experienced.

Lots of sailmakers have never cruised. They probably have done lots of racing and gained reputations from winning races. This does not necessarily prepare them for making bullet-proof cruising sails or understanding the problems of chafe and abuse that cruising sails are subjected to. Their primary concern is making fast sails to win races. Try to find a cruisers' sailmaker—one whose reputation is based on building worry free, highly durable, and long-lived sails designed for extended cruising. These sails can also be fast, good looking, and provide performance to satisfy even die-hard ex-racers. Your decisions on reefing systems, full battens/no battens, and roller furled mains should have input from a knowledgeable cruising sailmaker who can speak to the benefits and downside of each system. Two good cruising sailmakers are listed in Chapter 10, ***Contact Information.***

Furling the Jib

Until the development of roller furling systems, sailors would bring their boats into the wind to drop their jibs. This procedure made it easy to keep the jib on deck and to stow it into the bag. But with most boats now equipped with roller furling gear, sailors still bring their boats into the wind to furl the jib. This is no longer necessary, and in fact is not the best or easiest way to furl the headsail. It's a lot easier on the sail and the crew to put the boat on a broad reach, ease the sail, and then roll it in. It takes much less effort, does not flog the sail, and for most boats it does not even require using the winch. If you're caught in a squall, this technique can turn a Chinese fire drill into a controlled, seamanlike maneuver.

Whisker/Spinnaker Poles

You'll need a spinnaker or whisker pole to hold out the jib when going downwind—otherwise you just can't sail effective with the wind free. Lots of new cruisers avoid setting their poles off the wind because of reservations about putting it up and later having to take it down. But if they don't, the jib will flog and boat speed will suffer. The solution is to anticipate problems of setting the pole short-handed, and set up your boat to minimize these problems.

Mast-mounted whisker/spinnaker pole.

Mount your pole on the front side of the mast on a track. When not in use, the upper end of the pole slides up the track and the bottom end snaps into a fitting on the deck. In this position, it is always out of the way and never underfoot on the foredeck. In use, the pole is lowered, the outer end is clipped onto the furled jib sheet, and the pole is leveled horizontally with the topping lift. As the jib is unfurled and sheeted in, the pole will swing out and hold the jib in the wing-and-wing position. You will probably want to attach a foreguy from the outer end of the pole to a bow fitting, to hold it down and keep it from swinging around with the motion of the boat. During all maneuvers, the inboard end of the pole is always secured on the mast track, thus always under control.

When you want to take down the pole or jibe, reverse the procedure. As you ease the sheet, the pole will go forward and allow you to roll up the jib. Eventually, the pole will rest on the forestay with the jib furled. Release the pole from the sheet and then slide the inboard end back up the mast and snap the other end into its fitting on deck. If you want to jibe instead of stowing the pole, just dip the outer end of the pole to clear the headstay and clip it on the opposite sheet. Now just jibe the main and pull out the jib sheet on the opposite tack.

If you use roller furling and mount your pole on the front side of the mast, you can sail downwind with minimal effort and maintain complete control—even in strong winds. This procedure can also be used to reduce the size of the jib (or roll it up completely in a squall) without going forward and without leaving the cockpit.

If you're still a novice, take an experienced person with you and go out to practice on your own boat. Work out the procedures. Proper techniques will greatly simplify this process and ease any apprehension you might have about setting the whisker pole.

Anchors—Cruising Ground Tackle

You'll need extra anchors, chain, rode, shackles, swivels, and thimbles for cruising. Plan to carry at least five anchors (more are better) of two different types (one plow and one Danforth, for instance) and 250 to 300 feet of chain or nylon rode on the principle anchor. You should have at least one foot of chain for each foot of boat on all your other anchors. In very general terms, two of your working anchors should each approximate one pound of anchor per foot of boat, i.e. a 40-footer might carry a 45-pound working anchor with 40 feet of chain—err on the high side here. A storm anchor, if carried, should be heavier still. If you'll be cruising in coral waters, consider using all chain on the principle bow anchor. Coral is razor sharp and can saw through nylon rode in just minutes. Carry a dinghy anchor, too. One of those small folding grapnel-types works well to keep your dinghy from drifting away while you're diving or for keeping it off rough beaches and docks.

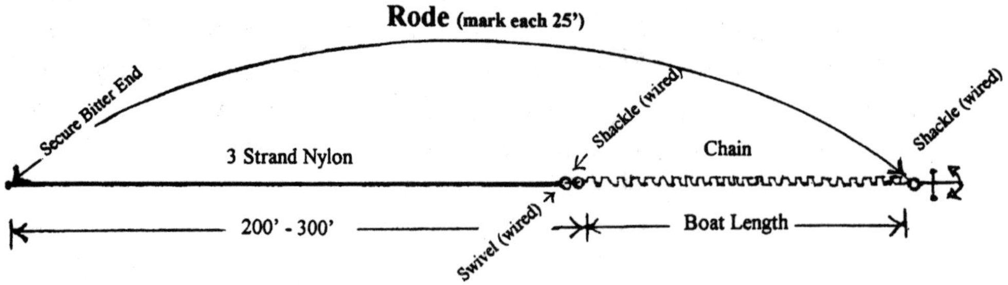

The following are equipment recommendations for a typical 40-foot cruising sailboat intended to be sailed mostly in mid latitudes. If you're not using an all-chain system, use three-strand nylon anchor rode for its increased stretch, ease of repair, and for easy splice-ability. If you use chain, triple-B (BBB) is the most commonly used chain for anchoring. To save weight in the bow of the boat without loosing strength, use *high-test* chain, but one size smaller than the correct BBB size. For instance use 5/16-inch high-test instead of 3/8-inch BBB. On boats larger or smaller than 40 feet, scale up (or down) the rode, chain, and anchor sizes. Wire all shackles closed with Monel wire. Use SS thimbles when attaching line to shackles. For powerboats, motorsailers, and multihulls you must consider the increased windage of their hulls when selecting suitable ground tackle. When cruising certain areas such as the Mediterranean, specialized anchors are sometimes needed for unique anchoring conditions. Check with cruisers who have returned from these areas.

Recommendations for a 40-foot sail or powerboat:

1) Principal bow anchor

A 45-pound CQR plow anchor (about 30% of cruisers carry a Bruce anchor on the bow) with swivel and 300 feet of 3/8-inch BBB chain; or a 45-pound CQR plow with 40 feet of 3/8-inch BBB chain with swivel and 260 feet of 5/8-inch to ¾-inch 3-strand nylon rode. The main anchor should be strong and versatile in many differing bottom conditions. More cruising boats use plow-type anchors than any other type.

2) Second bow anchor

A 25-pound Danforth-type anchor with 40 feet of 3/8-inch BBB chain with swivel and 260 feet of 5/8-inch 3-strand nylon rode. (West Marine's 25-pound Performance 20 anchor is high rated.) Because of its increased fluke area, this type of anchor can have as much holding power on good bottoms as heavier anchors of other types. These anchors can be bent, are best in sand and mud, and should not be used in rock or coral areas.

3) Stern Anchor

A 20-pound Danforth-type anchor with 40 feet of 3/8-inch BBB chain with swivel and 210 feet of 5/8-pound 3-strand nylon rode. This anchor should be small enough to be set and retrieved by dinghy when necessary. For years, I have used a 12-pound high-test Danforth with ½-inch rode for this purpose on a 37-foot sloop.

4) Backup Anchor/Storm Anchor

Carry an extra anchor similar to West Marine's highly rated Performance 35 or a Fortress (both Danforth-types). The aluminum Fortress anchor disassembles and stows readily in the bilge. Your backup anchor should be available for use in storms or in case your main anchor is lost or irretrievable. Put the chain (with shackle for connecting to the anchor) and a piece of seizing wire in a canvas shopping bag. Stow the chain with nylon rode attached (three to four coils made up with sea gaskets), so that all you need to do is shackle on the anchor and wire it closed. Keep it ready to go for emergencies.

5) Dinghy anchor

Typical dinghy anchor and bag.

Carry a small, folding grapnel anchor to use when you need to anchor the dinghy for diving or to hold it off the beach. A 5- to 8-pounder should be enough. Use about 10 feet of chain and 40 feet of ¼-inch line.

One of the best presents you can give yourself for peace of mind and the security of the boat is a good electric (or hydraulic) anchor windlass hauling an all-chain anchor rode. Its ease of use will encourage you to follow your best instincts and reset or move your anchor if weather or tide turn against you. Otherwise, the physical effort demanded to retrieve the anchor may dissuade you from taking action until it's too late. Buy one of those with an easy manual override, just in case. Anchoring with all chain will remove the worry of chafing through a nylon rode on unseen rocks or coral. See Chapter 8, ***Reference*—Anchors and Ground Tackle** for anchoring techniques and procedures.

Water Tankage

Many stock production boats do not come with sufficient water tankage for extended cruising. A passage to Polynesia from the U.S. West Coast or the Panama Canal could take up to a month before your first landfall. Watermakers now supplement the limited water tankage on many cruising boats. This is a good idea, but don't become totally reliant on this seemingly limitless source.

Any marine system can fail. While cruising for five years, I had to twice rebuild our PUR 12-volt watermaker—a complex job needing repair kits and spares. It had to be returned to the factory for more repairs. PUR says standard maintenance on that model is to rebuild every year of regular use.

Responding to cruisers' concerns about PUR's popular model 35, Recovery Engineering, Inc. developed a new SS upgrade for the plastic body, with fewer parts and a 3-year guarantee on all components. The new model 40 is about $2200, but the upgrade using your existing motor is $699. See Chapter 10, ***Contact Information.***

If your boat has limited capacity, consider adding additional tanks if space allows. Plan a good rain-water catchment system for your boat as a backup. Instruct each crew member on water usage and conservation. A few years ago, voyagers could cruise indefinitely on one to two gallons/person/day. Today that's considered very minimal. Lots of 2-person boats use eight to 10 gallons/day and more even when trying to conserve. Everyone on board must learn to ration water. Mid-sized cruising boats (33 to 45 feet) should try to get at least 100 gallons of water tankage, in addition to a good watermaker. If you don't want to install a watermaker, then start with at least 150 gallons for extensive cruising with two persons aboard.

The average mid-sized production boat has water tankage for 75 to 150 gallons. Salt water plumbed to the galley sink saves lots of fresh water and can be used for most galley duties—sometimes for cooking, too. Be wary of pressure water systems; they're particularly wasteful of water. For survival situations, you should have five to 10 gallons of water on deck in jerry jugs to toss into the life raft or sea for later retrieval. Leave a little air at the top of the jugs so they'll float. Jerry Jugs are good for hauling water from shore, as are the clear plastic, folding 5-gallon jugs. If you have a hot-water heater, there's another six to 12 gallons for emergency use. See Chapter 5, ***Departure Countdown*—Water Treatment,** and Chapter 7, ***Tropic Travel Tips*—Bathing and Hygiene.**

Fuel Tankage

Mid-sized production sailboats commonly have minimal diesel tankage (20 to 40 gallons) in the stock designs, so try to install additional permanent fuel tanks. These can be plumbed to provide an independent supply directly to your engine or, with a fuel-transfer pump, could be combined with the fuel in your main tank. This could supply a backup source of clean fuel, even if one of your other tanks is contaminated—sometimes a problem with third-world fuel supplies.

Sailboats—Many sailboat skippers achieve a cruising range of 500 miles or more under power. A Perkins 4-108/50 HP engine (a common auxiliary) uses ¾ to one gallon of fuel per hour at normal cruising speeds. If your boat cruises at 5½ to 6 knots, you would need at least 80 to 100 gallons in your tanks for a 500-mile range. If you're powering into head seas or strong winds, your engine will use more fuel and the hull speed will dramatically decrease. In the case of fuel tankage, more is always better.

Powerboats—Skippers wishing to cruise aboard powerboats should work to maximize cruising range by increasing permanent tankage and/or by using collapsible bladder tanks when necessary for longer passages. A cruising range of 500 or more miles would be adequate for most coastal cruising in the Americas.

Increasing Tankage--If you want to do some of the work of increasing the tankage yourself, start with a cardboard mockup of the tank in the exact shape and size to fit the space abailable aboard your boat. Tind a good marine metal fabricator who can do wondrous things in metal. (Use alumiinum for diesel tanks.) He will help you determine pickup points, breather locations, and clean-out hatches. At this point, you can also plan for installation of fuel gauges. It's now or never for this, or you'll forever be using a dip stick to measure your remaining fuel. (Heart Interface makes an excellent pneumatic unit called the TankTender: 800-446-6180.)

Electronics and Communications

Autopilots can steer your boat, radios can keep you in touch, depth sounders can alert you to underwater dangers, radars can tell of hazards far ahead or close at hand, computers can print weather maps and bulletins, and inverters can run all your shoreside convenience gadgets. Most modern cruisers rely heavily on marine electronics for navigation and communication. But don't go overboard with the black boxes. They can all fail—and generally do at the worst possible times. You need to have the skills, knowledge, and tools to safely sail and navigate your boat, even without your electronics—the old fashioned way. Back up your black boxes with compass, sextant, hand-bearing compass, lead line, good plotting techniques, adequate charts, and with regular and disciplined watch-keeping. Few extended cruises are completed without multiple electronic failures. Be prepared to do it the traditional way, just in case.

A list of desirable electronics (and they do make a cruiser's life so much easier) would certainly include the following: depth sounder, radar, GPS, EPIRB, autopilot, VHF radio (hand-held, too), laptop computer, single side band or amateur radio, 115-volt inverter, sailing instrumentation (wind-point/ wind-speed, etc.), and a weather-fax receiver or computer for gathering weather data. State-of-the art stuff might include: long-range or satellite communications that allow you to call or e-mail whenever you want, sonar that reads depths and objects ahead of the vessel, and integrated autopilots that use information from the radar and GPS to keep the boat on course. There are even entire electronic-chart systems that put hundreds of nautical charts on CD ROM, display them on your screen, warn you of dangers, continually update your boat's position, and feed all this information to the autopilot which steers the boat with the aid of the ship's integrated GPS receiver. There is also a weather-fax receiver that, when combined with a GPS, will plot the vessel's position within the displayed weather system and print it out. See Chapter 5, ***Departure Countdown*—Staying In Touch,** for more about these integrated systems.

Refrigeration

The four main types of marine refrigeration are as follows: 12-volt systems, 110-volt systems, mechanical (holding plates) systems, and gas (propane) units. There are also combination installations using two or three of the above.

Small propane solution to the "with or without refrigeration" question. Note the water-proof cover.

A large majority of people cruising today choose to go with refrigeration. Such was not always the case. Not long ago, crews sailing in remote areas purchased blocks of ice when available and carried them back to the boat for the pleasure of a cool drink or for food preservation. Some did without ice entirely. It's not as difficult as you might think. Many foods can be purchased canned or dehydrated that will last almost indefinitely. Some fresh foods can be preserved a long time when stored or wrapped properly.

Today's cruiser has the benefit of improved technology both in refrigeration equipment and in battery-charging capability. However, you must include refrigeration (along with autopilots and watermakers) as the most frequently repaired and serviced systems aboard a cruising boat. Add the requirements of refrigeration maintenance and the daily need to run the engine one to three hours to maintain the system, and you will begin to sense the necessary trade-offs for the crew. The required refrigeration maintenance, the noise and heat of the generator or engine to maintain the system or charge the batteries, and the restriction to stay near the boat while recharging should be carefully weighed to make sure they coincide with the cruising goals of the crew. All this may dilute considerably the pleasures of the ice cubes and cold beer.

With a refrigerator or freezer full of food, you cannot easily leave the boat for more than a few hours nor venture ashore for an interesting multi-day side trip should the opportunity present itself. In that case, you would have to make special arrangements to have someone monitor your refrigeration system in your absence, or empty the fridge while you're gone. In spite of the complications though, most boats start their cruise with refrigeration and do their best to keep it going.

On my first cruise to the South Pacific in the mid '70s, we went without refrigeration. We used dehydrated foods, TVP (textured vegetable protein), fruits and veggies that stowed well, and various techniques to store and preserve foods. That worked okay. Meals were satisfying but not great, and we all lost weight (low fat content). We learned to sail the boat really fast to the next cold beer and ice cream. In fact, beverages that had been stored in cans in the bilge were actually quite cool and refreshing. And after all, most of the native peoples in remote locations have never had refrigeration.

On our second cruise (five years to Central America, South America, and the Caribbean), we again started without refrigeration. But midway through a summer season in the Sea of Cortez, I changed my mind. During a visit to another boat, our host pulled cold beverages from a small box mounted in the cockpit. It was a travel-trailer unit built by Dometic available at trailer supply stores, and it ran on propane. One small 5-pound bottle ran it for a full month. We got one, had a waterproof cover made, and kept it outside, too. It worked great. In a strong wind the pilot would sometimes blow out, and in a squall it could flood out. But all in all, it required little attention. Dometic makes a quality unit that works on gas, 12 volts, and 110 volts (all three on each unit) and comes in several sizes. If installed below, it must be vented since is uses air when running on propane. It's another option to consider if you're on the fence about having refrigeration aboard and coping with the necessary maintenance it requires.

Generating Electricity

Most of the wonderful new equipment available to cruisers today requires electricity to run it. Fortunately, lots of it needs only small amounts of current which can be easily supplied by on board generating systems. Still, the modern cruiser is much more reliant on electricity than were voyagers of the past. When choosing equipment to put aboard the cruising boat, the skipper must be constantly aware how these new energy needs will be met.

Rail mounted solar panels.

When you run your engine (or generator), just as in a car you are generating electricity with the alternator for your systems' needs. Any excess energy is stored and saved in the ship's battery banks for future use. This balance between your electrical needs and the boat's generating capacity must be carefully weighed if you are to cruise without worry.

You can install high-output alternators or charge controls on the engine's present alternator that allow you to dial in your desired electrical output. But even these systems require running your engine—creating addition fuel usage, maintenance, and noise/heat in the process.

Swivel mount for solar panels.

Wind generators and solar panels can supplement the ship's alternator and sometimes largely fill the additional power needs of the vessel. Solar panels need sun, work silently, and require almost no maintenance—but they produce limited amounts of power. On the other hand, wind generators produce more energy, but they require wind and can be noisy. Some boats use both to good advantage. There are even trolled devices that generate electricity when you're underway. Talk with folks who have returned from areas you plan to cruise to determine the best solution for your boat. Do your homework before loading up on gear that may be unsuitable for the areas you want to cruise.

On bigger boats (42 feet and up) and on many powerboats, a diesel auxiliary generator can be installed to satisfy larger energy demands. But this, just like the ship's engine, means more running time, more maintenance, more fuel consumption, and more noise and heat.

When adding new equipment, the mariner must carefully consider the trade-offs of added convenience, utility, and comfort with the energy demands these added benefits require. For many experienced voyagers, the old advice to "keep it simple" is still a good rule to follow.

Dinghies and Outboards

Fast dinghies expand cruising horizons.

The selection of a proper dinghy—one that matches the cruising intentions of the crew—is an important consideration to maximize your enjoyment of cruising. Its importance can be compared to buying a new car at home—even more so. Your ability to get off the boat; to easily check in or out when in foreign countries; to travel from your immediate anchorage area for diving, fishing or exploration; to visit other boats; to set out additional anchors in a blow; to get ashore through the surf—all depend on your dinghy. The important factors to consider here are the number of crew that will use it, the size of the outboard motor to power it, how well it can be rowed, how heavy is it, whether it is rugged enough to survive serious cruising, and whether it will support the crew's planned interests and activities.

Cruising is very hard on dinghies. If you choose an inflatable tender, as most cruisers do, buy only the very best. It is a big mistake to economize here, as the elements will eat up some dinghy fabrics and delaminate others. The Avons, Achilles, and Caribs have shown they can survive even when continually exposed to the sun and salt. There may be others, but I have seen these three take it in cruising environments—they can handle the exposure to the elements and the abuse of cruising. See Chapter 8, ***Reference*—Dinghy Accessories and Landing Techniques.**

Hard Dinghies

Basically there are just two types of dinghies used by cruising sailors—hard dinghies and inflatables. The traditional hard dinghy (six to 12 feet) is made of wood, metal, or fiberglass and is still used by a small percentage of cruisers. It requires permanent stowage arrangements for passagemaking, such as davits off the stern or chocks on deck, to secure it on board. It is good for landing on rocky or coral beaches. Most hard dinghies are relatively heavy and row well. They can sometimes be converted to sailing dinghies (great fun), but are much less stable than inflatables when boarding from beach or boat. Many of these hard dinghies are rowed, or propelled by small outboards in the 1- to 5-HP range. Their basic hull design and the limited power provides deliberate speed, but generally it will not allow the boat to plane fast underway. This can limit your exploring range to only moderate distances from your anchored boat. Because the dinghy is hard, it can damage or chafe topsides unless carefully fendered when alongside your hull.

Inflatables

By far the most popular cruising tender is the inflatable dinghy. The inflatable has several basic variations in construction: the fully-inflatable model that rolls into a bag; another that has removable, inflatable, or roll-up floorboards; and the most recent one that has a permanent hard fiberglass bottom (RIBs) and only the side tubes inflate/deflate. The biggest advantage of an inflatable is its inherent stability which makes for easy boarding, and its light weight which makes for fast planing. These dinghies are great for exploring, fishing, diving, or just carrying supplies. For passagemaking, they can be fully or partially deflated and lashed almost anywhere on deck. With no hard or sharp edges to mar your bright work or topsides, they can be moored alongside without worry. With outboard motors in the 8- to 15-HP range, inflatable dinghies up to 12 feet can easily plane at speeds over 15 mph. Select a motor capable of planing your dinghy with your full crew and a load of provisions on board.

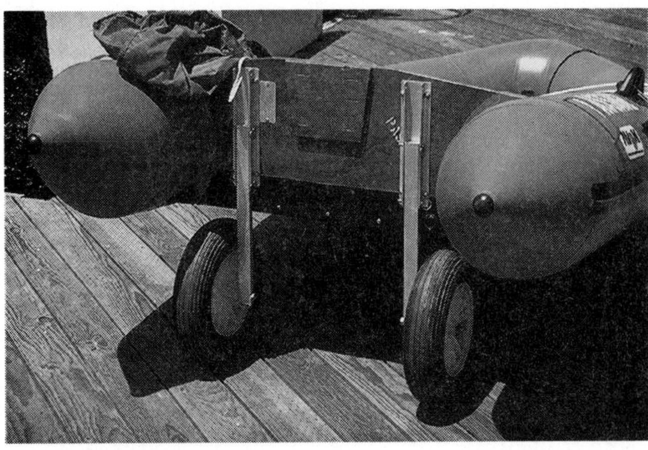

Mounted dinghy wheels - pin insertion model.

Dinghy Wheels

For landing through surf or just hauling the dink up a long beach, the addition of dinghy wheels is a boon to cruisers. Even the first mate single-handedly can pull a wheel-equipped dinghy high and dry when she takes the boat ashore. If the dinghy has a motor attached, no problem. Just drive it onto the beach and hop out. The wheels will protect the propeller and allow you to easily pull your tender beyond the surf and tidal range. Get the wheels with big 16-inch inflatable tires and carry a small bike pump to inflate them. With this model, you must lower the wheels and put in a locking pin as you approach the shore. Another type uses spring-loaded wheels that snap into place when lowered, which is easier to deploy. This model uses a smaller 10-inch wheel which may not extend deep enough to protect your propeller. Measure your dinghy and engine before making any purchase. See Chapter 8, ***Reference* - Dinghy Launching and Landing** for more information and for landing and launching procedures. See Chapter 10, ***Contact Information*—Supplies and Equipment** for source information.

A fast planing-type dinghy greatly increases the distance the crew can venture from the anchorage and enhances the fun of travel afloat. These dinghies generally do not row well, and although they are remarkably tough, they can be damaged by sharp coral and rocks. Some models can leave black marks on your topsides. These marks are annoying but easily removed. See Chapter 8, ***Reference* - Dinghy Accessories** for modifications to cruising dinghies such as towing bridals and lifting rings.

Tools

Every cruising boat needs a complete set of tools sufficient to handle all but the most major of engine repairs. You will need all kinds of hand tools, sockets (both U.S. and metric), end wrenches, Allen wrenches, punches, drill bits, taps to 3/8-inch, feeler gauges, files, etc. If you have installed an inverter aboard, then you can also take a 3/8-inch drill motor, saber saw, electric sander, and soldering iron. A portable vise, swaging tool, and cable cutters will certainly come in handy, as will gasket material in several thicknesses and O-rings of various size. Carefully inspect your onboard equipment to make sure you have covered all the bases. There is nothing more frustrating than to start a repair project only to discover you haven't the right tools to complete the job.

Self-steering—Autopilots

Once considered a luxury by purists, a reliable auxiliary method of steering is now considered nearly a must by the modern cruiser. Like the GPS, electric windlass, roller furling, and self-tailing winches, the autopilot is now thought to be essential equipment by most voyagers. Many units are electrical, but hydraulic models are also available. Some boats carry backup units, since autopilots are prone to failure from hard and constant use. The prospective cruiser will be wise to carefully research these units for the most suitable model for his cruising needs. Many electrical, cockpit-mounted, wheel units can be overpowered and become next to useless in heavy weather—just when you need them most. For most boats, the electrical autopilot is the most frequently repaired piece of electronic equipment on board. Heavy-duty hydraulic units are more powerful, but they are generally found only on powerboats or larger cruising sailboats. They are more expensive and require special hydraulic systems. Do your research and choose only the very best—go for the overkill here.

Self-steering—Wind Vanes

Monitor wind vane steering a cruising boat on a passage.

Curiously, wind vanes have been frequently overlooked since the advent of inexpensive electrical or electronic autopilots. That is too bad, because for many cruisers a wind vane will steer the boat when electrical units fail. In heavy weather, the wind vane is very powerful. Because it gets its power from the increasing wind and boat speed, it gets stronger as the wind builds. Since it does not use electricity, it doesn't draw down your batteries. It can be left to steer the boat indefinitely. It works best in consistent winds like the Trades, and least efficiently in variable weather where it follows the wind rather than a compass course. Wind vanes keep the boat on a consistent point of sail relative to the wind direction. If the wind changes direction, then so does the boat's course. Quite a few boats use both systems to good advantage—a vane when offshore where an accurate compass course is not required, an autopilot when inshore and a precise course is called for. Wind vanes frequently seen on cruising boats are the Monitor, Aries, and Hydrovane. On my own boat, we sailed with a Monitor vane and came to consider it a third crew member. Particularly in heavy weather, when the autopilot could have problems steering and might draw down the batteries, the wind vane performed powerfully and reliably.

Boat Insurance

If your boat isn't fully paid for, you don't have many options in the matter of boat insurance; you must remain fully insured (at least full-hull coverage) wherever you cruise. Cruising insurance can be expensive, can limit the areas where you can cruise, and can be restrictive as to the number of crew required to cruise your boat. For instance, you might have to carry an extra crew member for ocean passages.

Marine insurance seems to always be in a state of flux: coverage that was available last year is not available now, underwriting rules are constantly changed, and the company that wrote your marine insurance previously won't renew your policy for offshore voyaging. But, hang in there. There are always a few companies, some from overseas, that will underwrite mom and pop cruisers who are ready and well prepared. Do your homework early and ask other cruisers about their cruising insurance. Keep records of the marine classes and seminars you attend, and record the articles and marine books you read. You may need to document your preparation for cruising.

Another option could be a liability-only policy that protects your third-party liability. It does not provide hull protection for your own boat. This type of policy greatly reduces your insurance costs while still providing liability protection for other boats and marinas you might damage by accident or storm. If you plan to maintain real estate in the U.S. while you are cruising, inquire about an umbrella liability policy that would also cover your marine liability. This type of coverage can be quite inexpensive if the insurance company already provides your home or business coverage.

In any case, try to coordinate your insurance needs with a regular planned haul out of your boat. Marine insurers generally want a recent boat survey. If they need a complete out-of-water survey, the best time to do that is when you're going to be hauled out for bottom painting or other work. That way you can save the expense of a separate haul out just for the marine survey.

Currently, the three main carriers offering world-wide marine insurance for short-handed cruising are Blue Water Insurance, (also offering medical coverage for cruisers, 800-866-8906 in Ft. Lauderdale, FL), Lloyd's of London (many U.S. marine brokers can write this coverage), and Pantaenius (a German company with a British subsidiary—writes Atlantic and Mediterranean coverage: fax 011-411-1752-223-637). For more local cruising such as the Bahamas, Mexico, or the Caribbean, there are other companies including Boat/U.S. (800 283-2883) that can provide this coverage. West Marine insurance (800-937-8895) covers U.S. waters and limited Mexico coverage. They offer no Bahamian coverage at this time.

Spares, Spares, Spares

There may be some truth to the cruiser's lament that "if you have the spare parts aboard, you probably won't need them; but if you don't have them, you certainly will." Your last chance to put aboard easily available spare parts and repair kits at reasonable prices is before you leave the States. It will only get more difficult and expensive after you're underway.

Carefully inventory your boat and cruising gear. Get suggestions from other cruisers, diesel mechanics, and manufacturers. Get input from your crew in their areas of expertise. Lavish extra time on this chore—it will pay dividends. Get a parts kit and spares for anything that might fail—from galley faucet washers to a spare foot-operated pressure switch for your deck-mounted windlass.

No boat crew escapes the trauma of having equipment fail, only to find that needed parts are not onboard. I once spent four weeks in the Sea of Cortez, Mexico in August, wilting in the heat and unable to move, waiting for parts for my engine's raw water pump. I hadn't taken the time to properly check the spare parts invoice supplied by the manufacturer. The supplier had marked the shaft seal I now desperately needed as "back ordered" and I hadn't caught the omission before departure.

You do learn to improvise, to scrounge parts from other cruisers, and to rebuild broken equipment in third-world machine shops. But your forethought and planning before departure can save many awkward, inconvenient, and sometimes dangerous situations in the future. While you're at it, get service manuals for every piece of gear onboard. In Panama, we got our radar repaired only because we had the schematic and wiring diagrams for the unit to show the technician.

Guns and Weapons Aboard

Protection Underway

Many skippers struggle with the question of whether or not to carry weapons while cruising. Most decide the problems and negative consequences of carrying guns to foreign countries far outweigh any feelings of additional security. The countries you visit will most likely require that you declare and leave your weapons at your first port of entry. Your weapons can then be picked up when you check out to leave their country—but generally only from the original location. This will require you to return to the first port of entry which now could be many miles away and very inconvenient.

Should you decide to hide your weapons aboard and not declare them, the

consequences could be very severe if your guns are found in an inspection. In many countries this could mean imprisonment and loss of your vessel. For most cruisers, these are unacceptable risks for a marginal and theoretical advantage.

If you declare your weapons, the only time they would be available to you would be when you are on the high seas—a small percentage of the time.

Most times when you are approached at sea, the intruders are just curious and unarmed fishing boats wanting water, food, or just trying to sell you fish and sea food. These chance encounters can be scary though, because you are generally totally alone and far removed from other cruisers. Your unwanted visitors may outnumber your own crew, and their appearance can be very rough. In this situation, don't allow the visitors to come alongside until you are certain of their intentions. If you are under sail, start your engine for more maneuverability. Try to keep your stern to the unidentified vessel to reduce the number of potential boarders.

It is not unusual that some very strange looking boats can turn out to be military or naval vessels from the country you're visiting. Third-world navies sometimes use craft that don't look very military.

You can do several things at this point; you are not defenseless. Get the hand-held VHF on deck and have your mate start talking as if you are in contact with someone on the radio. Better yet, try to contact other boats and tell them the situation. If you make contact, tell them to notify authorities if you don't call back in an hour. Get the flare pistol ready, but out of sight. (A burning flare in the bottom of an open boat will make for a lot of confusion.) Make sure your kid-size baseball bats (which you carry for defense) are handy—and a machete, too, if you have one. Grab the large pepper-spray canisters (range 18 to 25 feet) you keep for self defense–like the product developed for protection from grizzly bears (*Counter Assault,* Missoula, MT 800-695-3394). You can even yell below, pretending to have addition crew members there. Should this situation occur at night, there is one additional defensive maneuver you can try. Turn off all lights aboard and try to go totally black to lose your pursuers. If you are otherwise invisible, most approaching boats will not have radar to track you.

If the approaching vessel is armed, you must conclude that it is a military craft. In any case, you would probably be no match for their firepower even if you did carry firearms. If they are military, you must yield to their requests to board. Generally this is nothing more than a routine inspection or training session for their crew. Be courteous and be prepared to show your ship's papers.

If you are at anchor and awake, you can still do most of the things mentioned above. If you are asleep, you could sprinkle tacks on decks, a la Joshua Slocum (because most intruders will be barefoot), or rig some sort of intruder alarm. Check at Radio Shack or Home Depot for 12-volt alarm systems. Motion-sensing lights and alarms are a good idea. These could be set to protect the boat and deter theft and intrusion even when you're ashore.

Protection Ashore

The smallest size pepper spray is just right for carrying in purses, money belts, or backpacks. It can be a strong deterrent to thieves, robbers, and pick-pockets when visiting big cities or traveling in the countryside. In Panama, a couple we know frightened off a man who had a knife, intent on robbery, simply by displaying their can of mace—a product not even as strong as pepper spray. Another incident, nearly comical, proves the effectiveness of these products. A friend of my wife's, while doing her laundry in town, had a small canister of mace roll out of her purse. A girl attendant picked it up to return it. Thinking it perfume, she gave herself a playful spray in the face. The result was about 20 minutes of profuse tears and intense discomfort!

Lightning Protection

Much has been written about lightning protection for cruising boats, but I've rarely seen much consensus on the steps one should take to reduce the risks of a lightning strike. The only agreement seems to be that cruising boats in the tropics during the rainy season or during squalls will most likely encounter extensive and potentially severe lightning storms. A boat struck by lightning could lose most or all of its electronics and electrical systems—a major loss. A worse-case scenario would have the through-hulls blown out and the boat sunk, though I don't know of such an instance. Preventive measures could include steering away from such highly visible storms if underway, and/or placing jumper cables or chains around the shrouds and dangle them into the sea—to provide a direct path to ground for the lightning strike. Some cruisers disconnect major electronics from the ship's electrical system during the storm. The list goes on and on, but the fact remains that there is little agreement as to what actually works. It has been suggested that a major strike can be so massive as to nullify any puny onboard attempts at diversion of such tremendous electrical energy.

Generally, damage is restricted to electrical and electronic components of the ships' equipment. This ranges from the masthead VHF antenna, to the starter and alternator on the engine, and everything in between—even equipment disconnected from the system! There are even reports of stored, spare electrical and electronic parts being damaged. A cruiser whose boat has been struck by lightning should also carefully check the mast and all standing rigging for damage—all the way to the masthead.

It is unusual for boats to be hit, but certainly not rare. Most cruisers have experienced such storms. Every season some boats will be hit and damaged. All the literature states that lightning seeks out tall things—like steeples in towns, trees in the field, or masts in an anchorage—as the path of least resistance to ground. On a boat equipped with an aluminum mast, the huge surge of electrical energy traveling down the mast and through the rigging could be drawn into the interior of the boat to do maximum damage to vessel, electronics, and crew.

To me, it seems the cruiser's first concern should be to avoid being struck. To accomplish this, the cruising boat may be well served by not providing the path of least resistance to ground, because by doing so you may bring on board the potential for damage and injury to boat and crew. To this end, do not use an ion-dispersing lightning rod that creates the path of least resistance. Do not throw chains around your shrouds and into the water for the same reason. But, in the final analysis, the choice is up to you. Mother nature is most unpredictable when it comes to lightning strikes. Without any protection you may decrease the possibility of being hit. But should the boat be struck, the potential for massive damage is perhaps greater.

There is an excellent small book on marine lightning called *Lightning and Boats* - by Michael V. Huck Jr., Seaworthy Publications, 1995. If you're headed for the tropics you may want to get a copy and consider his suggestions for protection as they pertain to your own vessel. His theories make distinction between boats underway and boats at anchor.

Two things should be done if you are in the vicinity of lightning strikes, however. The first is to put on dry shoes, socks, and gloves in order to provide as much insulation as possible. The second is to stay clear of metal objects (especially rigging) that could conduct the electrical energy to you if the boat should be hit.

Typical shade awning.

Boat Canvas

Until you go cruising, there are lots of things made from canvas that you just don't think about. There are cockpit spray curtains that make passages so much more comfortable. There are awnings of all sorts: Bimini awnings to protect the helmsman, and cockpit, full-deck, forward-hatch, and special sun awnings for the rest of the crew. There are awnings to keep the rain out and special awnings to catch water for the tanks. There are dinghy covers to protect your tender from the sun and rain. There are little canvas hammocks used to store fruit and veggies. There are, of course, the usual canvas protectors such as sail covers, hatch covers, binnacle covers, winch covers, and on and on. There are even special wind scoops to bring air into the boat—a must in the tropics.

Full sun cover is ideal in the tropics.

The most important of all is a good main cockpit dodger and Bimini to protect the crew when underway. These generally have lots of windows, maybe even one overhead that lets you check the sails when underway. This type of dodger is generally complex to design and sew. It is probably best left to the professional canvas worker, but I have seen excellent examples of cruiser-

Wind scoop on foreward hatch, cockpit Bimini aft.

sewn dodgers.

There are various canvas bags of all sorts and sizes to store and carry gear. We stored our dinghy anchor in a canvas bag that was convenient and always easy to grab. It also kept the points of the grapnel or small Danforth from putting a hole in the inflatable. Spear guns and Hawaiian slings fit in long canvas tubes. From 50 to 100 charts fit in a canvas sling that hung under the chart table. Back-up anchors can have their chain and rode neatly stowed in canvas bags. Stored this way, they are quickly and easily accessible when you need to get a second or third anchor out in a hurry. And finally, in the cockpit lockers and the lazarette, try slinging a piece of canvas, hemmed with bungee cord, from the overhead. You will be pleased with the amount of stuff you can keep from falling into the deepest recesses of your bilge.

BEFORE: Five-gallon jerry jugs in a stainless steel bracket, but sun can damage jugs.

AFTER: Canvas covers protect jugs from sun damage.

You can anticipate lots of your canvas needs before leaving and either have them professionally sewn or do them yourself—if your machine can sew canvas. Few home machines are heavy enough to handle several thicknesses of sailcloth or canvas. Once underway, you will find that some cruising boats carry machines capable of sail repair. Even if you decide not to carry such a machine yourself, at the very least carry some extra boat canvas and matching

Dacron thread—for the inevitable projects that come up.

Sail Repairs

Be prepared to make the necessary repairs to the boat's sails that continuous cruising will certainly require. Almost certainly there will be situations and circumstances that will chafe and damage your sails. This damage to your most vital pieces of cruising equipment must immediately be corrected, and you will have to make the repairs—at least until you make a landfall where you can find a professional sailmaker or canvas worker. Some cruisers travel with sewing machines that can sew canvas. Some of them also carry sailmaker's materials for repairing sails. But, unless you can find a pro, you will have to do it yourself by hand. To be ready for that eventuality, get a good book on canvas and sail repairs and clip articles on the subject as you see them in sailing magazines. Some marlinspike classes will include this kind of information, too. One good book on the subject is ***Canvas Work and Sail Repair*** by Don Casey, published by International Marine, 1996.

Carry a palm and needle, grommets, snaps, bees wax, stainless eyes, and D-rings too. Tell your sailmaker you're going cruising and have him set you up with a repair kit, including extra sail cloth and sticky-back material for sail and canvas repairs. If you want to save money, collect scraps of colored spinnaker cloth from your sailmaker to make the courtesy flags for the countries you visit. If you don't carry a sewing machine yourself but have the materials with you, you can probably find another yachtie who will do your various projects. If not, there are many places ashore in the third world that will reasonably and enthusiastically tackle your special needs.

Ship's Medical Kit

It is the skipper's responsibility to arrange for a suitable onboard medical kit. The contents may differ somewhat, depending on the type of cruise you've planned. The kit for a multi-year circumnavigation would certainly differ from one assembled for a two-week U.S. coastal cruise. Hopefully someone aboard has taken the time to carefully prepare for this

responsibility through personal study and by enrolling in a Medicine-At-Sea or similar course.

In Chapter 8, ***Reference*—Medical Kit**, you will find a listing of the drugs, medicines, and medical supplies assembled for long-range cruising by two different boats (50 to 55 feet)—the schooner Endurance and the sloop Victoria. Both boats were prepared for multi-year voyages. The skippers, Marv Miller and Jeff Thompson, used information from many sources including family doctors, Medicine-At-Sea classes, magazine articles, and seminars in assembling their vessels' medical kits. They then purchased their supplies, leaving the final acquisition of dated medicines and drugs until just before departure in order to extend the expiration dates and shelf life.

They assembled the documentation (prescriptions, drug descriptions and recommended dosages) for each medication. The next step was to protect the supplies from the marine environment by packaging them in watertight containers and plastic zip bags. The supplies were then stored aboard in a cool, dry place. Finally, they listed and cataloged all the ship's medicines and supplies for easy and fast reference. See Chapter 5, ***Departure Countdown*—Pre-Cruise Medical Procedures** for additional medical considerations such as immunizations and shots.

Ship's Library—Books, Tapes, CDs, and Videos

The acquisition of books, tapes, and videos is an important consideration when stocking and provisioning. In the past, traditional cruisers gathered up their favorite books—anticipating time to read as they never had ashore. Frequently that was true, and as the well read books accumulated on board, they hoped to meet others along the way to exchange and trade books. That is still true. But just as frequently, they now trade music tapes, CDs, and videos. Modern voyagers have more onboard entertainment options. Many boats have all the entertainment goodies they had at home.

I suspect, however, that you can overdo this aspect of cruising to the detriment of meeting local people, exploring new cultures, and making new cruising friends. Reach out to that guy on the other side of the anchorage—the new cruiser friends you make can be the best and most intense friendships you'll ever have. Row over, swim over, knock on the hull; that's often all it takes to start a meaningful longtime friendship. Make friends with local people, attend festivals and special events, go to church, take side trips ashore, ride on local buses. You won't regret it and will probably never forget it.

Recommended Onboard Reference Books

- *Boatowner's Mechanical Electrical Manual* - Nigel Calder.

◆*Refrigeration for Pleasureboats* - Nigel Calder.
◆*Diesel Engines* - Nigel Calder.
◆*The 12-Volt Doctor's Practical Handbook for the Boat's Electrical System* - Edgar J. Beyn, (Weems and Plath).
◆Equipment manuals and documentation for all equipment, electronics, and computer software.
◆Spanish/English, English/Spanish dictionary—if you're headed south.
◆Spanish phrase and vocabulary books. Language tapes.
◆French/English, English/French dictionary—for Polynesia and French-speaking countries. Take conversational French practice tapes, too.
◆Travel guide books and land maps for each area you will visit—tourist information. AAA-Auto Club, Fodor books, etc.
◆*Guide to Flags of the World* - Mario Talocci, (William Morrow and Co.).
◆*The Essential Knot Book* - Colin Jarmon, (International Marine). Shows just the basic knots, hitches, and bends necessary for cruising a small boat. Includes splicing techniques.
◆*The Morrow Guide to Knots* - Knots for sailing, fishing, camping, and climbing. It does not include splicing techniques.
◆*The Ship Captain's Medical Guide* - Dept. of Transport, (HMSO Publications). A medical book written expressly for voyagers at sea.
◆*Where There Is No Doctor* - Hesperian Foundation, 1992. If you're sailing remote areas of the globe, take this book too. It's not just a Medicine-at-Sea book.
◆Cookbooks—Take your favorite cookbook from home and also a good marine cookbook for cooking underway.
◆*The All New All Purpose - Joy of Cooking* (1997) - Rombauer & Rambauer Becker. Most popular all-purpose cookbook now includes lots of good information about seafood, including identification, cleaning, filleting, and cooking.
◆*Bottoms Up Cookery* - Leamer/Shaw/Ulrich, (Fathom Enterprises). For cleaning and cooking seafood. Probably out of print, but look around. Anna says that if you can find this one, it's a keeper.
◆*The Cruising Chef Cookbook, 2nd Edition* - Michael Greenwald. (Paradise Cay Pub.). Best general cookbook for cruisers. Includes tips for preparing for a voyage and provisioning in native markets.
◆*Keeping Food Fresh* - Janet Bailey, (Harper and Row 1989). Lots of good ideas for boaters about preserving fresh food.
◆*Survivor* - Michael Greenwald, (Paradise Cay Pub.). Excellent overview of survival experiences and techniques.
◆*Captain's Guide to Life Raft Survival* - Check with your marine bookstore.
◆*Canvas Work and Sail Repair* - Don Casey, (International Marine). Small, concise, with lots of pictures.

- ◆*Chapman Piloting and Seamanship* - Take a late edition, it's now in its 62nd. It has most of the reference material you'll need: weather, marlinspike, charts, rules of the road, lights, and lots, lots more.
- ◆*Boat Handling Under Power* - John Mellor, (Sheridan House). Techniques for handling cruising powerboats. Includes heavy weather procedures.
- ◆*Chart No. 1* - Available wherever you buy charts. U.S. government publication that lists abbreviations and symbols found on charts.
- ◆*Light List* - U.S. government publication that lists navigation lights for the region covered.
- ◆*Yachtsman's Emergency Handbook* - Hallander and Mertes, (Barns and Noble Bookstores). Great for emergencies onboard or in the life raft. All kinds of jury rigs, etc. What to do and how to handle damage control situations at sea. Book cover even glows in the dark so you can grab it fast!
- ◆*Heavy Weather Sailing* - K. Adlard Coles. Techniques for handling sailboats in rough weather; a classic.
- ◆*Cruising Ports: Florida to California via Panama, 3rd Edition* - John Rains, (Point Loma Publishing). Details cruising and fueling ports between the coasts. Much information for cruisers.
- ◆*Gentleman's Guide to Passages South, 5th edition* - Bruce Van Sant. If you are heading south from Florida, this is a "must" reference for passages and strategies.
- ◆*World Cruising Routes (3rd edition, 1995)* - Jimmy Cornell. Lots of vital passagemaking information required for extended cruisers. Details and lists international cruising routes for small craft. Includes timing and seasonality for each route.
- ◆Cruising Guides—for each area you expect to cruise. These guides provide much small boat cruising information not available elsewhere.
- ◆*Coral Reefs* - Eugene Kaplan. Highly informative—about coral reefs and the fish that inhabit them.
- ◆*Dangerous Marine Animals, 3rd Edition* - Bruce Halstead, (Cornell Maritime Press).
- ◆*Fishes of the Atlantic Coast* - Gar Goodson. Identifies fish from Canada to Brazil, including Bermuda, the Bahamas, Gulf of Mexico, and the Caribbean.
- ◆*The Serious Pacific Angler* - Ron Kovach, (Marketscope Books, 408-698-7535).
- ◆*Hook Up* - Charlie Davis, 11th reprint. So. California and Baja sportfishing. Fish identification. (West Marine has it.)

Nautical Charts

Even charts are going, or have gone, electronic. Scores of charts can now be stored on a single CD ROM computer disk and displayed on your screen. But it is risky to rely solely on this medium. I would not like to be totally reliant on anything electronic for all my charting or navigational needs—there is just too much chance of failure. There is still nothing as comforting as a good NOAA or DMA chart on your chart table or in the cockpit when you're making a landfall. That is not to say that modern electronics haven't shown some traditional charts to be inaccurate (up to a mile or two in charted positions), but this generally is in remote areas seldom visited by commercial traffic, and consequently there was little money or motivation for governments to update these charts.

To me, the amazing thing is the accuracy of these old charts and the diligence of early surveyors. Remember, many charts still in use today were first developed by conscientious cartographers and surveyors of an earlier time, using non-electronic means—no GPS, no satellites, and in some cases not even fathometers—just visual bearings and lead-line soundings.

Many voyagers leave the acquisition of their cruising charts until too late. With their departure imminent, they now concern themselves with the gathering of these vital navigational tools. With an unlimited budget, this may be less of a problem, as you can order what you need from a good U.S. chart dealer for about $15 each. If the charts are in stock, you can have immediate delivery. Charts, though, can represent a large chunk of your cruising budget!

The study and consideration of charts and related cruising materials has much to do with the success of an extended voyage. This planning stage can involve charts, chart catalogs, pilot charts, cruising guides, topographical maps, road maps, and any and all tourist information on the areas you're considering visiting.

On extended coastal cruises which are chart-intensive, you might need scores or perhaps hundreds of different charts to adequately cover your probable cruising area. Remember, too, you will need different scale charts—from small-area/large-scale harbor charts, all the way to large-area/small-scale sailing charts. On a cruise from California to Maine, our chart catalog numbered over 400 different charts and 21 cruising guides—and that was not an overkill. Many of those were used charts, purchased or borrowed from other cruisers who were then shore-bound.

The average price for used charts traded between cruisers is about $4 to $6. New, they are about $15 each. But, remember to question all navigational aids on these older charts if you are going this route; navigational aids probably will have changed.

I am not a big fan of photocopied charts, as they are generally reproduced in black and white and lose the significance of the original color. They also are not reproduced on the original high-quality chart paper that tolerates abuse, repeated folding, and even salt-water baths. I don't like, either, copies of charts that are reduced in size for easier handling. These charts frequently lose readability and utility in the process. A good compromise might be to buy new U.S. charts and guides for domestic waters—where information on navigational aids would be most helpful. But for charts of remote international areas, consider used charts if you can find them. Even old charts are generally adequate for most isolated locations.

You'll need lots of these - charts, chart guides, and cruising guides.

Although it is commonly attempted, don't count on copying or trading with other cruisers for the charts you need after you're underway. Do your own homework; acquire and thoroughly study your own charts prior to departure. Check the ads for used charts at the back of sailing magazines, the back of the SSCA Bulletin, or the Boat/U.S. magazine. Often you can buy whole sets for specific cruising areas. See Chapter 8, ***Reference*—Nautical Charts.**

Chart Guides

For some of your navigational needs, there are copies of U.S. government charts bound together as "chart guides." These are published by private firms and are almost exact duplicates of NOAA or DMA charts. Chart guides are the same as regular charts, but they may be reduced and sized for small boat use. Many charts appropriate for a certain geographical area have been bound together and are sold at bargain prices when compared to "official charts." In this collected form, they are handy to use even in the cockpit and should be considered for your cruise when ordering charts.

Cruising Guides

In the last few years, cruising guidebooks published by private parties have come a long way in replacing traditional government charts for many popular cruising locations. Designed specifically for small boats, they display lots of information relating to small craft not found on government publications. In addition, they display much the usual data found on familiar NOAA and DMA charts. Typically, they include information like details of harbors and anchorages specifically for small craft; the shoreside locations of boating services, stores, and government buildings; points of interest; and much more. In these guides, large-scale chartlets of popular cruising locales are included along with printed information about each anchorage or cruising location. Judicious buying of cruising guides, along with the careful selection of large-area (coastal and sailing) government charts, can do much to keep this portion of the cruising budget in check.

Chapter 5

Departure Countdown

(6 to 18 months before departure)

The Toughest Part

Many parts of your cruising preparation have probably been highly enjoyable. Each part completed led you one step closer to your departure goal. But, for the final months before leaving, you and your crew will be moving at a hectic pace to complete final projects, install the last pieces of equipment, provision the boat, and tie up loose ends ashore. Your last "to do" list will seem to be endless. You complete one project, cross it off your list, and then add two more. Your pace increases, but you feel you're losing ground. Almost all cruisers have had similar experiences. Don't despair, and don't expect to complete every item on the list. Some projects will have to wait and some will just not get done. Just go, do not delay. Hold a steady course for your planned departure. Cut those last ties that hold you on the shore—and commence living your cruising dreams.

At about this time, friends and relatives, having watched your feverish preparations, may have become a bit envious of your imminent departure. They will probably start asking if they can visit you somewhere en route. Perhaps they could join you for a few days of tropical sailing? Caution be advised. Your idyllic cruise can become the highly structured lifestyle you went cruising to escape. Concerns for the weather, lovely new anchorages to explore, rendezvousing with new cruiser friends, unexpected repairs, and a hundred other things could interfere with your keeping to a tight schedule in order to meet friends at some distant point. And quite frankly, friends and relatives may not easily fit on a boat that has grown much smaller since you've been underway—and is now just big enough for the two of you.

You can still meet your friends, but call them after your arrival in port and book them accommodations ashore if you have any doubts about their crew-worthiness or willingness to pitch in aboard the boat. If your boat is marine SSB or ham radio equipped, you can easily contact them to schedule visits and coordinate arrival details.

Cruising Routes

As your planned departure looms closer, you will need to give attention to possible itineraries and cruising time tables. Many passages have a seasonal component. They should be undertaken only during the correct time frames to maximize weather windows and to avoid adverse seasonal weather patterns. The overall cruise plan may be broken into several smaller sections, but on each section you must be mindful of the prevailing seasonal weather conditions for that particular leg. Pilot Charts and cruising guides of the area will be invaluable in making these important passagemaking decisions. Also, try to contact previous or present cruisers to the area for their onsite observations. Various marine radio nets, accessed with your SSB or ham radio, will be invaluable in tapping this resource.

Provisioning—by Anna Gleckler

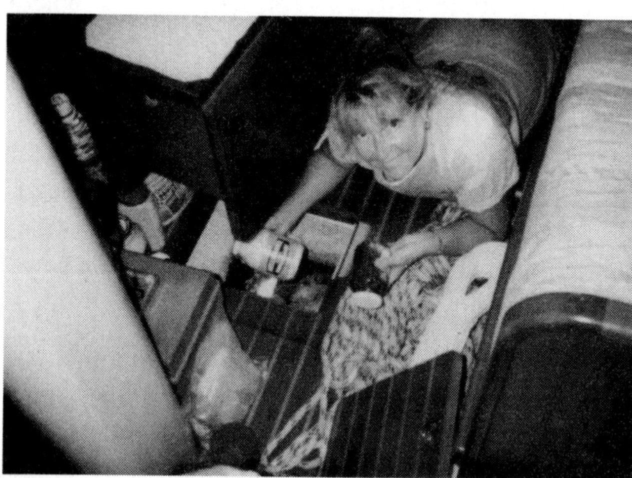

Some of "The Toughest Part."

Provisioning doesn't have to be an overwhelming or intimidating task. Depending on the duration of your voyage and whether it is in U.S. or foreign waters, provisioning for a cruise can vary from a trip to the supermarket (for a short coastal cruise) to a highly-detailed plan covering the vessel's needs for many months. Whatever your destination, you will probably start by making lists. What follows are the steps you can take to shop, stow, and prepare delicious meals for your life afloat. If you will address the following questions first, you can jump-start the whole process and reduce your anxiety toward this sometimes daunting responsibility. Ask yourself, for example:

How large is the crew?
What are their food preferences?
What is your cruising destination?
How long before the next provisioning port?
Will you have refrigeration?
Will you have a freezer?
Have you tailored your cruising menus?

Crew Size

Mom and pop crews are the easiest to plan for, since you will already know individual eating preferences and appetite levels. If you are sailing with additional crew, you will need input from each crew member before making up your shopping list.

Food Preferences

Determine the crew's food and beverage preferences before you start buying things. I love water-packed canned tuna and use it in lots of things at home, so I stocked a two- year supply when we went cruising. During our cruise, only once did I see water-packed tuna and then it was $4 a can! Walt likes cold beer in the tropics, but good local beer is available everywhere and it's fun to try them all—so you won't need to stow 10 cases of your favorite U.S. beer in the bilge. Don't load your boat down with provisions when they will be widely available where you are headed. The extra weight will adversely affect the performance of your boat and reduce its seaworthiness.

Are there any food allergies to be aware of? What size portions will you need to serve—large or small? These are things that probably will not change much just because you're on a boat. A 14-ounce can of corn will feed one big eater or four small eaters, but generally it will feed two average appetites.

If you are planning to buy products that you don't normally eat at home, be sure to taste-test them first before buying in bulk and loading up the boat. Every cruiser has horror stories about this common dilemma—cans and cans of something nobody on board can stand to eat! Your food preferences when in port will not change much just because you're on a boat. When you're underway, though, you will certainly eat more canned and packaged foods.

Overseas Availability

To some degree, your destination can play a part in your provisioning decisions. If you're crossing the Atlantic to the Mediterranean, you will be visiting

Fun shopping in local markets.

countries and ports where full resupply is generally easily accomplished. If you sail into the South Pacific, your passage will be long (up to a month), and resupply could be expensive and very limited on arrival. In the Caribbean, your passages will be shorter and resupply opportunities will vary from complete to marginal, depending on your destination.

We all have our favorite foods, spices, and other items that might not be available where we are going. For instance, I like adding a spoonful of difficult-to-find cream sherry to certain recipes, so I took a bottle of it cruising. It lasted for the full five years. Take horseradish sauce (hard to find) to mix with catsup (available everywhere) for making red seafood cocktail sauce for your crab and shrimp feasts. To find out what is available in your prospective cruising area, talk to experienced cruisers who have been there and read cruising literature, boating articles, or provisioning books. Join the Seven Seas Cruising Association ($29 a year. Ft. Lauderdale, 954-463-2431) to receive their monthly bulletin that includes letters from cruising sailors throughout the world, and which often includes this kind of on-site information. The radio nets are a good source of information once you're underway and listening regularly.

Fiji street vendors with strange new produce.

Remember, people in other countries eat, too. Almost every country, except possibly on remote islands, will have basic staples such as coffee, pasta, flour, rice, yeast, cooking oil, instant milk, cheese, basic canned foods, and other condiments. Fresh foods like potatoes, cabbage, carrots, green peppers, and onions were generally available. Beer and soft drinks (except for diet drinks) are everywhere. Wine is frequently hard to find, of poor quality, and (when available) can be more expensive than in the U.S. Gin, vodka, whisky, and Scotch were expensive and often hard to get. You will probably learn to enjoy rum and tequila if you cruise in the Americas—both are cheap, always available, and seem to go with the climate. There are often good local liquors in every cruising locale. Fresh meat and fish are available, but with meat you may not recognize the cuts—just point to the piece you want. In Central America, filet mignon (called Lomo Fino) sold for $1 a pound and other cuts were even cheaper. Guatemala has hot dogs, and Colombia has great hamburgers.

Items that were expensive or not commonly available were: refined white sugar, rich-tasting chocolate, whole wheat flour, packaged one-meal mixes, instant rice, instant foods, canned water-packed tuna, sweet pickle relish, and good canned meats.

Cruise Length

Whether you are just leaving from your home port—or reprovisioning in a foreign location—you must consider the time period until you will be at the next provisioning port. When you're finally there, will it be a local fruit and veggie stand, an outdoor public market, or a complete supermarket with a good selection of foods and supplies?

Local fish market.

With or Without Refrigeration

Most voyagers today start their cruises with refrigeration and probably also freezers. There is nothing like the tinkle of ice in your drink when you're sailing in the tropics. But there is a price. Marine refrigeration equipment requires much more of your attention than your reliable old fridge at home. Not only is there increased maintenance, but there is the daily need to monitor the system and recharge it as necessary. Generally this requires running the vessel's engine an hour or two every day—sometimes more. The other negative is that this daily responsibility to maintain your system can restrict your ability to visit and travel ashore. The majority of cruisers seem to work this out and find compromises they can live with.

Just a few years ago, most long term voyages were accomplished without refrigeration. You can eat well without it—and lots of cruisers still do. Some cruisers use ice, but block ice is often either not available or requires hauling to get it to the boat—a sometimes tedious task. Even if you have a refrigerator onboard, it's a good idea to learn how to preserve foods without it. As a backup, learn the techniques of waxing cheese, brining butter, making jerky, preserving bread with vinegar, coating eggs, pressure canning, and how to dry foods. See Chapter 8 - ***Reference*** - **Preserving Food** for details. Then if you lose your refrigeration, or just your patience with the required maintenance routine, it won't end your cruise. If you're planning a long cruise or circumnavigation, especially if you're on a minimal budget, going without refrigeration may make a lot of sense.

Gathering Menus and Recipes

When planning and collecting menus, I focused on dinner. Breakfast and lunch menus seem more standardized and can be frequently repeated. Therefore, my planned menus stressed the evening meal. I had about 30 different dinner menus, most of which were one-pot or casserole types, but used fresh foods when these were available.

There are many good cookbooks written for cruising (see Chapter 4, ***Outfitting Your Vessel For Cruising*—Ship's Library**), but surprisingly, many times your favorite cookbooks and recipes from home are just as suitable when used on the boat. You don't need to grossly change your eating habits to go cruising, but you do need to consider onboard space limitations. On most boats there is not enough space for a library of cookbooks.

The solution is to make your own cruising cookbook, which on my boat I call my *Galley Bible.* Long before departure, gather up and copy all your favorite recipes from the many cookbooks and sources you use on a regular basis ashore. Insert them into a loose-leaf notebook with dividers. Use index tabs to make sections for *Recipes, Product Information, Inventory Lists*, and *Equivalents and Substitutions*.

Divide and label the *Recipe Section* with tabs to create categories to suit your needs, for example: *Appetizers, Baked Goods, Bisquick Recipes, Breakfast Menus, Casseroles, Desserts, Dinner Menus, Fish, Heavy Weather Menus, Lunch Menus, Meats, Potluck Ideas, Sauces,* and *Snacks.*

The section for *Product Information* will contain manufacturer information and the labels from food products removed from their original containers. Some products should be repackaged for better stowing aboard—like cornmeal, instant mashed potatoes, and Bisquick.

The *Inventory List* should describe all the foods and non-food items you have aboard. Make a diagram of all the ship's storage locations, name or number each locker, and list what's stored there. Then as you use things up, you must keep track of what's remaining. If you're conscientious, you might even keep track of when your provisions were first purchased. To avoid loss, you might try to eat up your oldest provisions first.

For the *Equivalent and Substitution* section, just copy this from your best cookbook. There are many excellent lists. Get one that includes metric measures and conversions too—you'll need it!

During the last year before departure, each time you use a favorite recipe make a point of copying it and putting it in your *Galley Bible.* That way, it won't ever be a big chore to find the recipe you need, and you will end up with your best menus on the boat. Besides your *Bible,* you will probably want to take one complete reference cookbook like *The All New All Purpose Joy of Cooking,* along with one cruising-type cookbook such as Michael Greenwald's *The Cruising Chef, 2nd Edition.* And don't forget a good fish book that tells you how to catch, clean, and prepare a variety of seafood.

There should still be storage room left for a few of those small and excellent product-cookbooks from Bisquick, Philadelphia Cream Cheese, Campbell's Soup, and Fleishman's Yeast.

Tailoring Your Menus

Create menus that fit the varying conditions of cruising. If you're sailing in rough weather, you will need simple one-can or one-pot meals perhaps using a package mix. While underway, plan meals that only need boiling water to prepare. Cup O'Noodles, instant soups, or instant oatmeal work well here. Include instant drinks like packets of coffee and cocoa. In bad weather or for overnight passages, keep a push-top thermos filled with boiling water in your deep galley sink and near a closable container with instant food and snacks. For those midnight snacks, have another container for granola bars, candy bars, peanuts, cheese and crackers, salami, popcorn, and cookies.

If you're in port at a marina, you will have access to most fresh foods and supplies. You can fix your favorite menus from home. And when the boat is anchored in a pristine lagoon, you may have time to bake bread, cakes or other goodies.

At home, we never ate canned corned-beef hash, canned tamales, or canned fruits and veggies. But we did when we were at sea or at anchor. They were convenient and fast to prepare. In port, we ate only fresh foods similar to our previous eating habits ashore.

Shopping—by Anna Gleckler

The lists of what to buy come from the preferences of the crew, modified by the need to prepare meals on a cruising boat—sometimes underway and sometimes in rough weather. How much to buy is simple mathematics. For example, figure out the number of times you expect to serve eggs on your upcoming passage. Multiply that by the number of crew and then add the number of eggs you will use for baking. Do this for all the ingredients in every meal. Don't forget your paper products and staples. Your guestimate will be accurate enough to keep you from wildly over- or under-estimating your needs.

Taste-test every product you plan to buy in case lots or bulk. Be willing to spend more for quality and convenience products. Organize your shopping list by food categories and items will be easier to find in unfamiliar markets.

Shop for (and stow) your stores and provisions days, weeks, and months ahead of departure. At home each time you go to the market, purchase a few items from your master provisioning list. Start with the heavy and bulky items like beer, sodas, canned foods, paper towels, and toilet paper. Since you are buying well ahead of departure, you can take advantage of special buys and sale items. Keep them in the trunk of your car. Each time you visit the boat, unload the car and stow these items on the boat. By the time you are ready to cast off, you will have only the perishable items and ice to load aboard.

Stowing--by Anna Gleckler

Provisioning and stowing will go on for the weeks and months before departure. All the food and supplies so carefully selected and dearly paid for must now be stowed board. First they must be protected from the marine environment and then cataloged so you can easily find them when needed.

Provisions must be sealed and protected to remain usable and palatable. The elements (salt water, fresh water, air, sun) and critters (roaches, weevils, ants, rats!) will try to rob you of precious supplies, but you can generally win this battle if you have prepared properly and remain alert.

You'll use a lot of zip baggies, vacuum bags, Tupperware, duct tape, bubble wrap, and maybe Kerr and Ball canning jars, too. The things that absolutely must be protected from moisture and humidity should be stowed in glass containers (wrap them in newspapers or stuff them in a sock to prevent breakage). Even Tupperware yields to the tropical, marine environment sooner or later. Stow the things that need to stay dry as high as possible; stow the heavy things low with extra protection. Some cruisers still use varnish on their cans, but not many anymore—unless they will be out for a very long time without the opportunity to resupply.

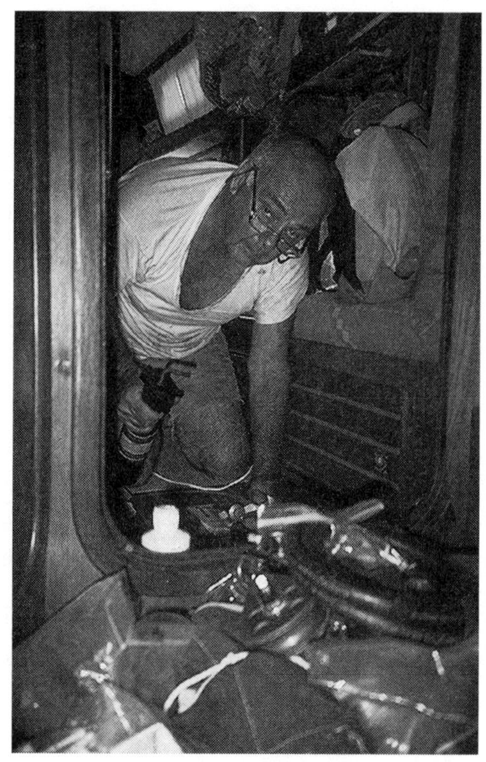

Spares, spares, spares.

Finally, make a diagram of your boat's storage lockers and then number or name each one. Then, as each item is placed aboard, it must be cataloged in your master file immediately—before it disappears forever. It is amazing and frustrating how quickly and completely you can lose things on a small boat. Every inch of storage space will eventually be filled. Remember, as you consume your stores and use your spare parts, you must also log this into your records, or you won't know what you have left!

Organizing The Galley--by Anna Gleckler

What galley equipment will I need aboard?

If you have been living aboard for a while before departure, you will probably already know most of what is necessary to equip the galley for cruising. Galley needs for a boat are not much different than living ashore. You may be able to bring much of the equipment you need from home. A good shake-down cruise will further refine your selection. For some boats, it may be necessary to down-size certain galley equipment in order to fit in galley sinks or in the stove's oven. You will probably be eating lots more seafood than when you were shore-based. Take good filleting knives and a tenderizing hammer to deal with these delicacies from the sea. A pressure cooker may be something you don't use at home, but it sure comes in handy afloat to contain hot foods securely in the pot, to save on fuel (because it cooks much faster), to reduce cabin heat (because of faster cooking times), and to transfer food by dinghy (spill free) to another boat for a pot-luck dinner.

Is the stove gimbaled? Does it have fiddle rails and pot holders?

Any time the boat is underway, and sometimes at anchor, you'll be happy that the stove is free to swing independently from the motion of the boat. A well-gimbaled stove will keep the cooking surface horizontal most of the time and avoid spills. Many times you will also want to use individual pot holders to secure pans on the stove top. This will prevent them from sliding about and spilling when the boat moves too quickly. Always cook with covers on the pans for the additional protection.

Good things from small ovens.

Does the stove have an oven? How big?

You'll need an oven for extended cruising—no way around it. But don't be surprised if it doesn't work just like the one at home. You may have to light it with a match, and you may have to turn your food around in the middle of the baking cycle to get even baking. When purchasing pots and pans, be sure to size them for your onboard oven. Chances are it's much smaller than what you're used to at home. If you're cruising on a small boat without a built-in oven, stove-top baking in a tightly sealed pot or pressure cooker can substitute quite well. In this case, you will need an asbestos pad (flame tamer) under the cooker for best results.

What is the ship's fresh water usage?

We found that most of the ship's water usage occurs in the galley—so attention to conserving water should be concentrated there. The other area of extensive use can be in the shower. If you can train the crew to use fresh water only for rinsing, after bathing in salt water, you will much more likely control excessive and wasteful fresh-water usage. A fresh-water rinse can be done with only a quart or two of water. If you have limited tankage (less than 150 gallons for 2-person crews), if the passage is long, or if you haven't installed a watermaker, everyone on board will have to become very conscious of water conservation.

Is salt water plumbed to the galley sink?

If you install a manual or pressure salt-water pump in the galley, you can reduce fresh-water usage by half. At sea or in clean anchorages, use salt water for all galley duties, including washing fruits and veggies.

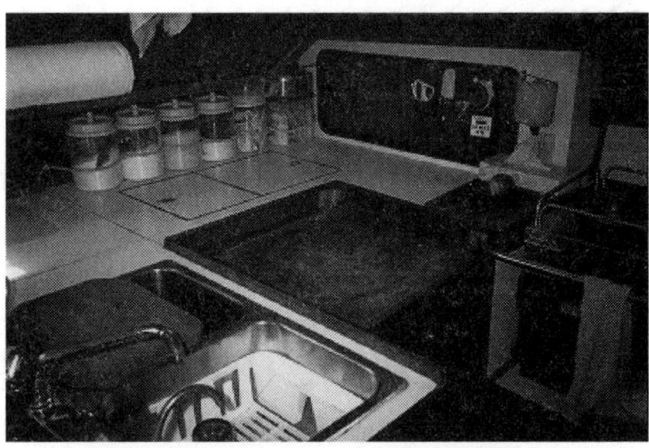

This galley has sinks with salt/fresh water, sliding bread board, counter-top storage units, paper towel rack, cutting board on sink, and a gimballed stove.

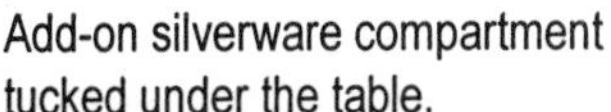

Add-on silverware compartment tucked under the table.

Are deep sinks set into the counter top?

Sinks in cruising boats should be deep (7 to 11 inches), to avoid splashing water about the galley in a seaway or when on a heel. You're blessed if you have double sinks, as you can always find a use for the second one when doing dishes or as a place to set a hot pan from the stove. If your boat doesn't have deep sinks, consider an upgrade—it's not a major undertaking. If you're handy, you can do it yourself. See Chapter 3, ***Finding Your Dream Boat*—Purchase Considerations—Galleys.**

Stowing Mechanical Spare Parts

To protect mechanical parts, tools, and spares, I had good luck spraying them with Boeshield, LPS#3, or Lanocote (West Marine or Boat/U.S.). These products leave a thick, long-lasting coating that protects from rust and corrosion. Heavy spare parts were stowed in the lowest parts of the boat and wrapped in old towels intentionally made oily. Finally, they were placed in sealed plastic bags, and stowed in canvas bags tied with drawstrings. Use Boeshield, Lanocote, and LPS#3 on everything mechanical which might have a tendency to corrode—like your engine, outboard motor, windvane, etc. Use these products above and below decks; they will cut down on your maintenance problems and save your gear. They will provide protective, semi-hard barriers that stand up to salt water, but they are not true lubricants as such.

Water Treatment and Storage

Watermakers have cut down on the need to carry large amounts of water. Many modern cruising sailboats of moderate size carry only 100 to 150 gallons of water in their permanent tanks. Prospective cruisers figure to top-off their tanks when needed with the watermaker and collect rain water when available. However, the watermaker is one of the "most-frequently repaired" pieces of equipment onboard. It requires regular maintenance and needs to be "pickled" (flushed with sodium bisulfite) when not in regular use. This is a simple but important process of cleaning and preserving the membrane. You will need to educate the crew on careful water usage, and don't become totally reliant on your watermaker.

Water stored for extended periods in your tanks can go bad and smell worse. It is important to treat your tanks on each fill-up with Clorox bleach (liquid is easiest to use) to prevent unwanted bacterial growth in the tank and hoses. This will kill any organisms in the water and keep your boat's water clean and safe. The formula is one ounce (2 Tbsp.) of bleach per 50 gallons of water. This ratio is sometimes hard to calculate when you top off partially-filled tanks, so many cruisers add Clorox until they can just begin to smell it in the tap water. The smell eventually evaporates out. I have heard of people who add a bottle of white wine to remove the smell, but I can't personally vouch for the success of that. Any water taken on board from sources ashore should be considered "suspect" and treated with Clorox bleach to avoid problems. (You can also add 2% iodine at 3 Tbs. per 50 gallons instead of bleach.) After treatment, allow a few hours for the Clorox or iodine to work before using the water.

Here are two other old-water rules: 1) to freshen old water, add a bottle of wine (any color) for each 50 to 100 gallons, and 2) to keep water from going stale, add ½ cup of baking soda per 50 gallons when you fill the tanks.

Staying In Touch

It used to be that after you cast off, you became almost instantly inaccessible to the rest of the world. Depending on your perspective, that was either a plus or a minus for the cruising experience. It still takes very few offshore miles to eliminate the distractions of TV and AM radio. But your ability to communicate over long distances, once confined to the use of marine SSB radios and amateur (ham) radio equipment, has significantly changed. Now you can access satellites for fax, e-mail, and weather reports if you desire—perhaps to the detriment of your new laid-back cruising style. The newest technology is still expensive, but costs are dropping quickly.

Very High Frequency (VHF)

VHF radios ($175 to $800) are for line-of-sight (short range) communications. They are small, inexpensive, require no special licensing other than your FCC-assigned call sign, and are available in permanent-mount and hand-held models. For cruising U.S. coastal waters, they can provide communication between boats, between you and the Coast Guard, and between you and the bridge-keeper when cruising the waterway. In a remote anchorage when the crew takes off in the dinghy, a small hand-held unit can provide a life line to the mother ship. VHF radios are indispensable for gathering local weather information in U.S. waters. Even when you're beyond the range of U.S. shore-based stations, VHFs will still provide ship-to-ship emergency communications.

Although you no longer need a VHF license for U.S. waters, boats in international waters (or boats over 65 feet sailing anywhere) need a valid radio license from the FCC. When cruising overseas, you may be required to prove you are legally licensed by the FCC to operate your radios. If you need a license, get an application form from any electronics dealer. There is no charge to obtain a license. If you prefer, call the FCC at 888-CALL FCC.

Marine Single Side Band (SSB)

If you don't have special communication needs, the simplest way to stay in touch with folks back home is still with marine SSB (or all-frequency ham) radio through AT&T's high seas operators. Three stateside stations—one in California (KMI), one in New Jersey (WOO), and one in Florida (NMN)—provide this service. Call AT&T at 800-SEA-CALL for information. You will need to establish your account with them before departure to avoid having to give out your credit card number over the air. For ham radio operators, phone patches to folks at home are often available through shore-based hams if you have a *general class* license or above.

SSB radios are used for both ship-to-ship and ship-to-shore calls. These radios permanently mount somewhere aboard your vessel and are priced between $900 and $2200. They are capable of long-range, high-seas communications. With marine SSB you can talk on marine nets, communicate with other cruisers, and also receive marine weather information. When using marine SSB, you are not limited to personal correspondence, as in amateur radio communication, but you may transact any necessary business matters over the air. By using AT&T high seas operators and your SSB radio, you can call home for $4.98 per minute. It is best to set up a marine account with AT&T before departure.

With another method that uses AT&T's new service High Seas Direct, you can direct dial to almost any phone in the world for just $1.29 per minute. This new service also provides privacy on the air, but does require about $1000 in special equipment (handset and modem) for your boat. This service is the least-expensive way (after equipment purchase) to communicate by voice to shoreside locations. High Seas Direct does not yet provide e-mail connections. For information, call AT&T High Seas Direct at 800-392-2067.

Amateur Radio (Ham - Single Side Band)

Ham radio operation is an honored tradition on the radio bands. It is a great international fraternity of amateur operators, both male and female, who communicate world-wide on frequencies reserved for amateur radio. Hams provide communications in natural disasters, marine emergencies, and offer two-way communications for far-flung cruisers and people stationed overseas. On these bands, some hams can "patch" you into the phone lines so you can talk with friends and relatives back home at no charge to you. Any phone charges are paid by the shore station receiving your call.

As per FCC rules, communication on these bands cannot be commercial in nature. In other words, you cannot conduct business over the air. Ham licensing requires study and a bit of diligence. But once gained, it opens communication routes to other cruising and shore-based hams, to weather information, and to many marine nets. For emergencies, most ham radios can also access AT&T services mentioned above.

Don't wait until the last minute to get your ham license. You'll need six months to a year to study the technical portion and learn the Morse code. But you will not regret the time spent to earn your license. Ham radios are priced a bit less than the SSB units mentioned above. Request information on amateur radio testing and licensing from the American Radio Relay League (ARRL) at 800-326-3942, or fax them at 860-594-0259. The Gordon West Radio School (714-549-5000) provides study tapes and materials, in addition to weekend seminars, to help mariners prepare for amateur radio licensing exams. Hundreds of cruisers have received their ham radio licenses by studying Radio School materials and/or attending the weekend seminars.

Ham Radio Nets (SSB WX)

From our own cruising experiences here are the ham radio nets we used most frequently. You will need a license to participate, but anyone can listen in. The times are GMT/UTC/Z (Greenwich Mean Time/Universal Coordinated Time/Zulu Time).

Net Name/Location	UTC Time		Frequency
Mexico:			
Sonrisa Net	1400 UTC		3.968
Chubasco Net	1445 UTC		7.294
Baja Net	1500 UTC		7.238
Manana Net	1900 UTC		14.340
Pacific Maritime Net	2200 UTC		21.402
Intercontinental Net (Pacific & Hawaii)	24 Hours		14.300
Central America:			
Central American Breakfast Club Net (for cruisers south of 20° N.)	1300 UTC		7.085
Pacific Maritime Net	2200 UTC		21.402
Intercontinental Net (Pacific & Hawaii)	24 Hours		14.300
East Coast/ICW/Bahamas/Caribbean:			
Eastern Caribbean Waterway Net	1345 UTC		3.968
Caribbean Maritime Mobile Net	1100 UTC		7.237
Northwest Caribbean Net	1400 UTC		4.054
East Coast Waterway Net	1245 UTC		7.268
Trans Atlantic Maritime Mobil Net	1300 UTC		21.400
Weather—All Areas (SSB)			
Southbound II (Herb Hilgenberg)	2230 UTC	6A	6.224
Herb is an expert amateur forecaster for all areas. He starts on 6A then switches to 12A.	Continuation	12A	12.353

E-Mail Communication—Satellite and High Frequency Systems

Satellite communication systems are immune to the occasional interference and propagation problems of SSB and ham radios. Because it is new technology, it is more expensive. However, competition will ensure lower prices as multiple new services come on line.

Inmarsat C is a bit expensive for many cruising budgets—from about $4000 to $5000 for Trimble Navigation's dome-receiver (mounted on your deck)

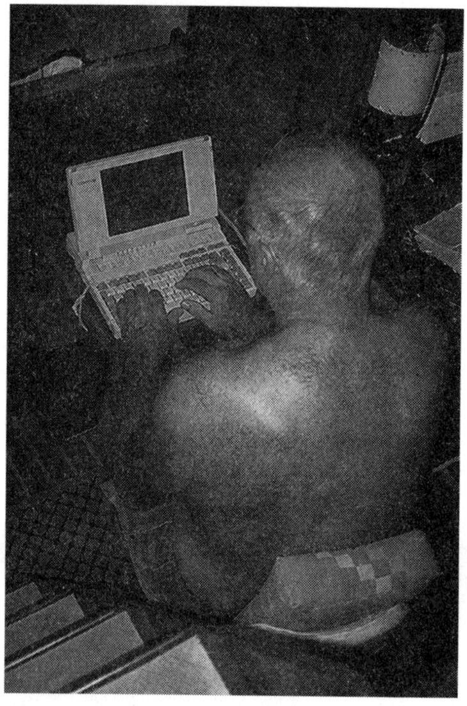

Correspondence, weather, even e-mail on board.

and the below-deck electronic unit. There are additional transmit/receive charges. But this satellite system allows 24-hour e-mail access anywhere in the world. You can also send fax, telex, correspondence, and distress calls—but not voice. For an additional charge, the service also provides personalized weather reports for specific locations. The basic system includes the same highly-reliable distress capability used by round-the-world race boats (Comsat Mobile Communications, 800-424-9152).

There is also a world-wide network of land-based HF radio transmitters that can provide low cost e-mail service. All you need is your high-seas radio, a computer, and the necessary software.

Non-satellite, high-frequency radio services are also now available for the cruiser who needs offshore communication. P-Sea Mail ($129 from Software Systems Consulting, San Clemente, CA) is a software program that uses your onboard computer, a proprietary modem connection to your radio, and a world-wide system of shore-based transmitting stations to provide services using radio frequencies. The software also has weather-gathering capability through the National Weather Service. This program utilizes your ham or SSB radio for transmissions to shore-based stations which then utilizes the Internet for e-mail. It requires no additional hardware, and for a monthly charge of $19.95 you can send about 1000 words a month to multiple recipients—before incurring additional word charges. (Software Systems Consulting, 714-498-5784).

PinOak Digital Corporation in New Jersey (800-PIN-OAK1) uses 22 frequencies on your SSB radio (no ham radios) to provide 24-hour world-wide communication. Your computer connects (utilizing their special modem) to the SSB radio, which then connects to shore-based stations to complete the connection to the internet for e-mail. Because of radio propagation characteristics, cruisers in remote areas can sometimes have reduced hours of service availability. Regional weather reports are available from NOAA, and two private weather services are available at extra costs. The initial cost of $1995 includes all necessary hardware and software to interface with you computer. There is then an annual fee of $275, plus receive/transmit charges of 95 cents per 1000 characters.

The above two systems are not without a learning curve. They require study and some radio expertise. While they are not push-button operations for the novice, they can be learned by the serious mariner needing immediate hookup or links ashore.

A system that uses a laptop computer, with a PC-card modem and an acoustic coupler, is the absolute cheapest way to send and receive e-mail when cruising. Subscribe to an internet provider like CompuServe (just over $9 a month) and use local access numbers in the countries you're visiting. Then when you are ashore, set up the laptop and hook the acoustic coupler to the telephone receiver to send e-mail messages and receive any waiting mail. The cost of a modem and coupler should be less than $200. This service works, obviously, only when you're ashore and local phone service is available—even pay phones. Check at any computer store for the modem and acoustic coupler. For an internet provider contact CompuServe, P. O. Box 20212, Columbus, OH, 800-336-6823.

Magellan's GSC-100 accesses low earth orbiting satellites for global e-mail.

Magellan Satellite Navigation, known for its hand-held GPS units, has just announced two new systems that will be of interest to cruisers concerned about global and offshore communications. Their *GSC 100* is the first hand-held Global Satellite Communicator. It provides world-wide e-mail capabilities through a system of low earth-orbiting satellites. It became available in late 1997 and retails for about $1500. It features an integrated GPS receiver to identify your position, plot courses, and store waypoints.

The second unit is called *World Phone* and looks something like a small 5-pound computer with a telephone handset. It provides world-wide voice, fax, and data communications. *World Phone* uses Inmarsat mini-M service to provide voice communication at less then $3 a minute. The portable electronic unit on the boat will retail for under $4000. (Magellan Systems, San Dimas, CA, 909-394-7050)

Technology for world-wide communications is changing so fast that within a couple of years it will be possible to use a cell phone aboard your boat

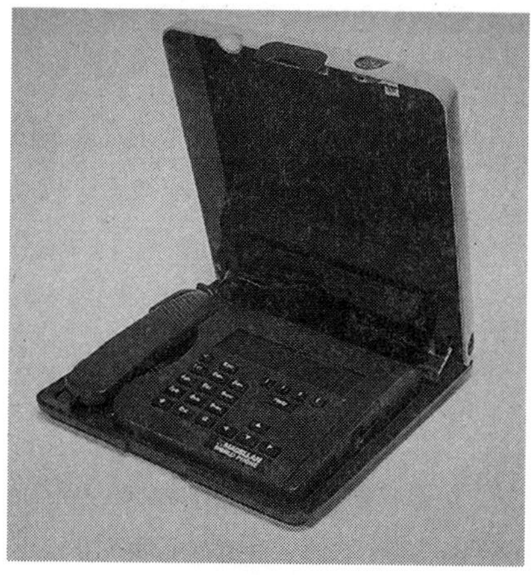

World Phone provides world-wide voice, fax, and data.

anywhere in the world. The new global systems use satellites in low earth orbit. These are already being launched. If you don't need these services right now, wait one or two years for the new satellite systems to get the bugs sorted out and come down in price. Satellite links to the internet and shore-based phone systems are almost here.

Mailing Services

Frequently overlooked in the last-minute rush to embark on your long-pursued dream to cruise is the need to retain a lifeline to shore—for those loose ends that will continue to haunt you, and for the communications you'd like to maintain. Even if you've sold the house, the car, and closed your bank accounts, you will probably need to retain a home base for the inevitable mail, correspondence, and bills that seem to be unending. Some cruisers leave a relative in charge and use their mailing address while cruising. In some cases, you might want to also leave a limited power-of-attorney with them as well. But relatives may quickly tire of a job that has grown larger than they had anticipated. Bills to pay, checks to deposit, mail to forward, spare parts to order, messages to take—all this might be more than they bargained for.

The other approach is to maintain communications through a professional mailing service that provides this kind of support. Some mailing services are operated by former cruisers who fully understand your needs. Do you want mail forwarded, bills paid, checks deposited, boat parts ordered? Mailing services offer various levels of support for the voyager. Their job is to deal with the correspondence needs of travelers and cruisers like yourself. A number of these services have been handling the needs of cruisers for years with economy and dispatch.

Depending on the services you need, the basic fees range from $10 to $30 a month. For taking messages, forwarding packages, monitoring e-mail, or bill paying there will be additional charges. The February, 1997 issue of *Cruising World* magazine published an informative article by Faun Skyles on this subject called *The Check's In the Mail.* It would be a good place to start if you will need a mailing service while you're gone. The companies listed below offer specifically tailored services such as buying parts, forwarding mail, and VHF, SSB, or satellite links. There may be others.

◆*Blue Skies* - 328 45th St. Court West, Palmetto FL 34221, 800-729-4591.

◆*Cruising Services* - PO Box 119031, Hialeah, FL 33011, 800-326-1023.

◆*Mail Call* - 2726 Shelter Island Dr., San Diego, CA 92106, 619-222-1186.

◆*Professional Agents* - Alief, TX 77411-1209.

◆*St. Brendans Isle* - 60 Canterbury Ct., Orange Park, FL 32065, 800-544-2132.

◆*TOCO* - PO Box 501179, Marathon, FL 33050, 800-678-7639.

◆*Voyagers' Service* - 88005 Overseas Hwy. #9, Islamorada, FL 33036, 800-860-9256.

Finances

The almost universal use of credit cards has greatly simplified the problems of financing your cruising. No more do you need letters of credit, certified checks, or even traveler's checks for that matter. With just a Visa and/or Master Card (Gold cards are probably best.), you can tap your U.S. funds from anywhere in the world. Use your credit cards for cash advances. Sometimes local banks put limits on the amount you can withdraw on each cash advance. In Cartagena, Colombia for instance, they had a limit of $400 per transaction. So you may have to get more than one cash advance to get sufficient funds for your needs. Carry both Visa and Master Card, as some banks work with just one or the other. Some cruisers also have good luck with American Express. They have offices in many cities, and because they have local addresses—unlike cruising sailors—they can be helpful in receiving correspondence or packages.

If you use your credit card for other expenditures ashore, watch it like a hawk. Don't let it out of your sight. There are lots of stories of how cards have been used for several imprints without the cardholder's knowledge. Of course you find out about this much later, when you finally see a statement of your credit card transactions—long after you have sailed away. This is why you must check you credit card statements every three months—the grace period allowed by the credit card companies for any disputed claim against your account.

You must also concern yourself with the exchange rate from U.S. dollars to the local currency. This can vary widely from store to store, or restaurant to restaurant, and rarely to your advantage. Before making your purchases, check the exchange rate. Make sure it corresponds closely with the locally quoted bank rates.

In addition to cash advances, we tried to always carry $200 to $300 in one-dollar bills aboard the boat. The U.S. one-dollar bill is widely accepted—even in small villages—as proper payment for goods and services. Larger denominations are not as widely used and may not be accepted. The village fisherman alongside your boat wants $3 for his lobsters and he doesn't have change for your $10. So keep a good supply of ones available. Depending on your itinerary and lifestyle, you might also want to conceal additional ready funds in larger-denomination U.S. bills. Carry some traveler's checks aboard for emergencies, too.

Safety Drills—Overboard Procedures

An important part of final departure preparations must certainly be developing an awareness that emergencies and accidents can happen at sea. These incidents actually are quite rare for cruising boats, but you and your crew's reactions must be pre-planned and focused should emergencies occur. Man-overboard situations, fires and explosions, accidents, sinkings, and boarding threats about cover the array of scary things that could happen.

All safety systems must be understood and their use demonstrated to every crew member. Attend a safety-at-sea seminar to see liferafts deployed, flares shot off, fires extinguished, and overboard crew recovered. Then on your own boat carefully go over these situations with your own crew using your own equipment. Rehearse procedures until everyone is comfortable. This single step will do much to relieve crew anxiety.

Good safety harnesses and well engineered jack lines (safety lines led from the bow to the cockpit) can do much to keep the crew on board, even in bad weather. These need not be rigged permanently, but can be set up before each offshore leg. Try to rig your jack lines so they are not underfoot and not themselves the source of accidents. Some skippers find that nylon or dacron webbing, rather than round line, works best. Webbing prevents rolling and slipping if you should accidentally step on your jack line when moving about the deck. In heavy weather and at night, every crew member on deck should wear a safety harness and shoes. They should immediately "hook up" when coming on deck.

Fishing Gear And Trolling

If you're not a fisherman, it doesn't take long to appreciate and eventually envy those who always seem to have good luck "pulling a line" while underway. VHF radio accounts of their triumphs attack the salivary glands and bring sly looks from the first mate. Comments like "Honey, I wish we could do that!" are sometime heard from below decks just as she opens another can of corned-beef hash. And it gets worse if Joe, the fisherman, later dinghies around the anchorage offering gifts from the deep—while he laments, "I can't get it all in my freezer."

Barracuda can carry ciguatera toxin, so test before eating.

Before your stateside departure, do some research and prepare for this eventuality by putting aboard the necessary tools and gear to complete a first-rate fishing setup for a cruising boat. This need not be expensive equipment, but it certainly will include line, poles, reels, hooks, sinkers, lures, and the incidental stuff to put it all together. Take along a good fishing book written about fishing underway. Get another book that identifies fish and seafood and tells how to catch, clean, and prepare these delicacies. And talk to the experts on your dock—those guys with the sportfisher down the gangway—you know, the guys you never speak to. They know fishing like you know sailing!

Hawaiian slings can be fun and productive.

While you're at it, get some snorkel gear (mast, snorkel, and fins) and a Hawaiian sling or spear gun for your underwater adventuring. If you are going to the tropics you may be able to skip the wet suit.

You should also know that fishing gear of all kinds makes excellent trade items in the third world. So stock up on fishing basics—especially hooks and line. Even if you don't hook up, you can always trade with the locals for your dinner!

Safety Gear

Now that you've made the commitment to cruise, it's time to accumulate the safety gear that you may need to protect the crew underway. This is another area where you will need to use discretion. Do your research to determine your own real needs and comfort level. You can spend lots and lots of money on safety equipment. Life rafts, EPIRBs, flares, personal GPSs, personal watermakers, man-overboard retrieval systems, survival suits, harnesses, and all kinds of specialized survival gear. The lists go on and on for gear you hope you will never have to use. Add to this list special heavy-weather sails, drogues, and parachute sea-anchors, and you begin to see the problem.

Talk with cruisers who have recently returned from their adventures to get

Deck-mounted liferaft can be locked at anchor.

Liferaft under waterproof sun cover is protected from damage.

first-hand and realistic opinions on what they think is really required. Ideally you'd like to have it all, but realistically, buying it all would probably sink the boat and the cruising kitty, too. If your cruise is limited in scope and is of relatively short duration, you may be able to rent some of the equipment you'll need. Most crews would opt to have all the safety stuff, but costs, maintenance, and stowage problems must be considered. Ultimately, you will find the right compromises that will keep you within your cruising budget.

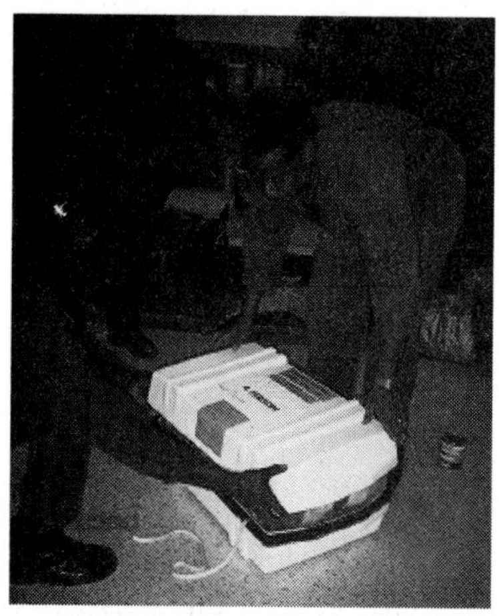

Liferaft repack in Trinidad.

Abandon Ship—The Ditch Bag

Every boat crew needs to prepare for a worst-case scenario—a "what if" situation. Because of that possibility, we buy life rafts, hand-operated watermakers and much, much more. Before departure, one last thing you need to do is prepare an abandon-ship bag or ditch bag—something you can grab in the last minutes that contains the absolutely essential things you must have if you are forced to abandon ship. These are the things that couldn't be included because of space limitations within the sealed life raft itself.

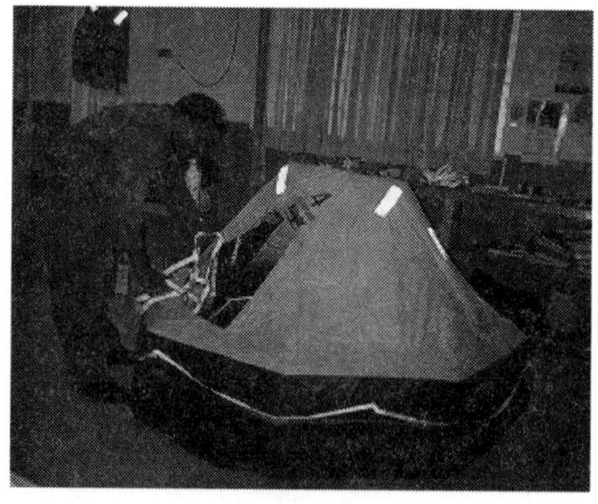

Avon 4-man liferaft inflated, looks small!

Not much room inside: just first aid kit, flashlight, paddle, flares, food, water, and drogue. Prepare a ditch bag, too.

When you toss your ditch bag overboard it must float, be waterproof, and have an attached, brightly colored, floating, polypropylene line (30 feet) to facilitate retrieval when the crew is in the life raft. You should also be prepared to throw overboard two 5-gallon water jugs attached with the same kind of polypropylene line. Leave enough air in each jug so they will float. Hopefully, you were able to include one of those hand-operated watermakers in your life raft (*Pur Survivor*, model 06, $585, 800-787-3347) when it was repacked. When you get the water jugs and ditch bag safely aboard the life raft, you should have most of what is necessary for survival. See Chapter 8, ***Reference* - Ditch Bag,** for a list of ditch bag contents.

Camera Equipment

For extensive cruising, most folks take cameras and film (extra batteries, too), anticipating opportunities to photograph beautiful places they will probably never visit again. If you plan an extended cruise, particularly in the tropics, you should be aware of certain problems that relate to exposing film and cameras to the marine environment. First, you will need to take lots of film with you, because it may be unavailable (or very expensive) where you're going. If you can, refrigerate (but don't freeze) the film to prolong its useful life. Otherwise search out the coolest spot in the boat and keep your film there. We kept 35mm slide film without refrigeration for several months in the tropics and processed it only when we returned to the States for visits. Until you can get exposed film processed, store it in the original moisture-proof plastic container. Only once did we lose film to the heat and humidity—two rolls turned mottled green and the slides were unusable. Store your cameras, film, and equipment with silica packets to absorb the moisture.

If you cruise with other boats, you may find opportunities to send your film home for processing when other cruisers returning to the U.S. for visits. On the marine radio nets, you will frequently hear of people returning home who are willing to take other boaters' mail and film with them. The sooner exposed film is processed, the better, but in this case, you won't have the opportunity to check your pictures to see how the camera is operating. Pick your film couriers carefully; you don't want to lose the irreplaceable shots of your adventures to an unreliable person who doesn't follow through. Make sure you get his/her stateside address, just in case.

In the tropics, cameras with lots of electronics seem more susceptible to failure than some older models with more mechanical components. Low-tech sometimes is more rugged in this environment. After you've been cruising awhile, your camera lens should be removed from the camera body and inspected. Open the aperture wide and hold it up to a light. Because of the humidity, fungus can grow inside the lens and slowly degrade all the pictures taken with that lens. If the lens is not perfectly clear and it looks like tiny cracked eggshells on portions of the lens, that's fungus and you must have it serviced and cleaned. That will probably require sending it back to the States for disassembly. This kind of expertise is frequently not available in the third world. On three occasions I had to have lenses cleaned and serviced while we were cruising. Unfortunately, I had already lost one-of-a-kind pictures to the gradually deteriorating image quality.

To get the best cruising pictures, you should buy a polarizing filter to remove the reflection so often apparent in marine scenes. It works the same way as your Polaroid sun glasses and lets the camera see the scene without glare—it makes colors vibrant and rich. It is a two-part filter, which is rotated until you see the best picture. As you revolve the lens on the camera, you can see the remarkable difference it makes. Except for reduced light and flash shots, you can leave the filter on for all your shots.

If you want to take underwater pictures, you'll need a special underwater camera. Any camera used for underwater photography must have a flash—otherwise your pictures will be all blues and greens. All the brilliant colors of tropical fish and corals will be lost just a few feet below the surface. The flash provides the sunlight needed below the surface to photograph these scenes. If you are a scuba diver, then buy the best. Get a Nikonos V—it can go wherever you dive, even to 160 feet. It is a top end camera and will cost up to $900 for the body and lens. Nikon has a new model RS which will soon replace the Nikonos V. The separate strobe on these cameras is extra.

If you just want to take snorkeling pictures down to 15 feet or so, then you have several choices of less expensive cameras that have underwater capabilities. They have built-in flashes and can take the pictures you want for either slide presentations or scrapbooks. Look at the Canon Prima AS-1, the Minolta Weathermatic, and Konica's Mermaid. All three are automatics and will serve both above and below the surface. Expect to pay between $300 and $400 for these models.

If you have only a passing interest in underwater photography, then get a disposable camera. Both Kodak and Konica make models for about $15 that will work down to 10 feet or so. These models use 400 ASA print film and have a built-in flash. Both take surprisingly good snapshots, but not slides.

Cruising Gifts

Frequently overlooked in the last hectic days of stowing and provisioning are gifts to share with the local inhabitants and the kids you meet along the way. You may think you're cruising on a shoestring, but almost everywhere you go in the third world, you will find that you have far more of the world's material blessings than the local folk. Take a little time to collect some cruising "give-aways" before you fill up those very last storage lockers. Your thoughtfulness now can make for beautiful and moving experiences throughout your cruise. Almost anything you have in abundance could be used for gifts to the locals. Gather up the old toys from the grandchildren, children's used clothes (always a winner), colorful T-shirts, caps and hats, wind breakers and sweaters, writing paper and pens, fishing knives and gear, hooks and line, snorkeling gear and flippers, picture books and magazines—the gift list is endless. And don't forget food, soft drinks, medicines, and even old reading glasses!

In Central and South America, we saw a real modern Pied Piper. A thoughtful cruiser had brought hundreds of colored balloons. He had learned to inflate them and make animals for the kids in the villages—just like the circus clowns. He created a sensation wherever he stopped.

Just before our own departure, Dan, a good friend and former college tennis coach, gave us 300 used green tennis balls which we threw to kids wherever we went. It was a great door-opener and once created one of the most moving experiences of our cruising. We had anchored in a small remote cove on the island of Dominica in the Caribbean. It was off a small and very poor village. As the kids swam or paddled by that day, we would throw them a green tennis ball—to their great delight.

The next morning, I was just hauling anchor when we observed a man climbing over the rocks at the side of the cove and coming toward us. He was carrying what looked like an awkward and heavy sack of citrus fruit. When he was just opposite our boat, he carefully took off his clothes and placed them on the rocks. Now down to his skivvies, he entered the water with his bag of fruit and started swimming toward us. By now I had stowed the anchor. With the motor idling we waited for the lone swimmer to arrive. For him it was long and hard swim, because of the load he was carrying and because he knew we were leaving. When he finally arrived he was breathless, but it soon became obvious that what he wanted was one of those green tennis balls for his young son at home. He didn't expect a gift. He had brought the only thing he had to trade—his grapefruit. Later, with moist eyes, we watched him as he swam slowly back to shore with his green treasure—back to the rocks where he redressed and started proudly back to his village.

Paperwork—Ship's Papers

If you're going cruising to escape the necessity of dealing with governmental entities and mounds of paperwork, you may be disappointed. Yes, you will generally get to talk to live people rather than listen to recorded messages (as frequently happens here in the States), but there is still the necessity to deal with officialdom wherever you cruise.

Certainly all members of the crew will need valid passports. Check the expiration dates. Make sure the date on each passport extends well beyond the end of your cruise; otherwise you will have to find an American Consulate or Embassy to renew the passport even while cruising remote areas. Many island nations and small cities do not have handy consulates or embassies to service cruising sailors. An expired passport might necessitate an inconvenient and unwelcome sail to find someplace to renew it.

If you are now cruising and have a passport that will need renewal during your cruise, try to get it renewed while you are back in the States for a visit. If you explain the situation, you may be successful. Ask them to rush it through, since you will probably not want to stay away from the boat too long. Currently, new passports require proof of citizenship, an I. D. and two passport photos (2" x 2"). The cost is $65 dollars. Renewals are $55, and expedited service is an additional $30 bucks. Kids under 18 are $40.

Incidentally, carry extra passport photos and copies of your passport with you while cruising. They will come in handy if you do have to renew, or if your passport is lost or stolen while you're cruising. Having extra photos and a copy of a lost passport will greatly speed the replacement process at any U.S. Consulate abroad.

Checking In and Checking Out

When visiting a new country, you will have to clear in and out at an official port-of-entry. Only certain entry ports will have the necessary official manpower to process your paperwork. From the marine radio nets and by talking with other cruisers in the area, you can often determine the best place to clear in and out. In Spanish-speaking countries, you will need to visit the Port Captain (Capitan del Puerto), immigration (Migracion), customs (Aduana), and sometimes a health officer—generally in that order, but it can change from place to place. These offices are frequently not close together and may require a long walk, or a bus or taxi ride, to complete your paperwork. Sometimes one official does the work of all three.

Third world official "check in."

Procedures can change from country to country and from port to port. Sometimes officials want to inspect the boat and sometimes not. Sometimes they have their own boat and will board you after you are anchored; sometimes you must meet them ashore and transfer them from the dock to your boat in your dinghy. Sometimes they complete all paperwork aboard the boat; sometimes they want only the skipper to appear at their office with the boat and crew's official papers—while the crew remains aboard. If you're staying for only 24 hours at an anchorage, you can request to check in and check out at the same time—saving you time on departure day.

Sometimes the entire crew must present themselves at the appropriate office. In every case, though, you will need each of the crew's passports and visas, the vessel's registration or document, and your clearance papers from the previous port or last country visited. In Latin America, if you are checking out and all your papers are in order, you will be given a ***"despacho"***—a clearance to another port in the same country. If you said you are sailing to a port in another country, you will be issued a ***"zarpe"*** to that country. You must have these official clearance papers to check in at your next landfall.

In Mexico, you will also need the boat's crew list. You can make up your own crew list or use the one printed in several cruising guides. It should include the vessel's identification details: boat name, home port, document or registration numbers, net and gross tonnage, U.S. port of departure, and your furthest-planned Mexican destination. Then list details about each crew member (include children and guests), such as name, age, citizenship, and passport number. If anything changes, you must start over with a new list—don't just cross out items or names. Make lots of copies of all documents; in Mexico you will need them every time you check in or out.

You will also need to complete tourist cards/visas for each person onboard. Fill out forms at the Migracion Office in Mexico or obtain them in the U.S. in advance. Procure fishing licenses for the vessel, the dinghy, and each crew member from many stateside fishing stores, or the Mexican office of Pesca at 2550 Fifth Ave., San Diego. Their phone number is 619-233-6956. Call for information. Get the fishing licenses before departure.

Visas/Tourist Cards

Many countries allow you to obtain tourist visas when you arrive in their country. Others want cruisers to have obtained their visas before arriving. Inquire before leaving your last port-of-call as to the requirements of the country you're headed for. Much of this type of information will be available to you by listening to the marine radio nets and by asking other cruisers you meet. If you're in the States, inquire from the country's embassy or consulate for the information you need.

Documentation

You must have proof of ownership for your vessel. That may be either U.S. Coast Guard documentation or state registration. If your vessel is documented to a corporation, you may need a letter from a corporate officer authorizing your use of the vessel. Have it on board just in case. Generally speaking, your boat should be documented if you plan an extended cruise. Additionally, if your boat is financed, your bank will most likely require the vessel be documented if sailing abroad. It shows the boat as a U.S. vessel. Carry several photocopies of your ship's document or state registration with you. They will come in handy when checking in and out.

Each year while cruising, you must make arrangements to have the documentation renewal sticker sent to you before your document expires. If you're home for a visit prior to the renewal date of your document (or within 30 days after the renewal date), you can request a renewal form (800-799-8362, opt #5) from the USCG National Vessel Documentation Center in West

Virginia. (State USCG offices don't do this anymore.) They can fax the form to you; when completed, you can fax it back. But you will then have to wait for regular mail to receive your decal. You do not need to have your original document home with you; just the document number is necessary. You can request renewal forms even if your document has not yet expired. Your new document, in that case, will run for 12 months from the date it was renewed. Don't let your document expire. If it goes 30 days past the renewal date, you will have to complete the entire documentation process again!

If your vessel is not documented—but rather state registered—then you may have problems in some foreign countries. France, for one, (and certain third world nations) does not accept vessels with state registration as readily as it does those with U.S. documentation. You may have complications and more paperwork checking in and checking out.

For a fee, many boaters have the documentation process completed by private firms. But the new simplified version for recreational boats is now only one page long, and can easily be completed by cruisers wishing to do their own paperwork. Your vessel must be at least five gross tons to qualify. Request an application by calling 800-799-8362. Or you can write to USCG National Vessel Documentation Center, 2039 Stonewall Jackson Dr. (Dept. 1111 for renewals), Falling Waters, WV 25419-9502.

Fishing Licenses

Not all countries require fishing licenses for cruising sailors. You need to inquire locally about this. Mexico is an important exception, though. You will need fishing licenses for each crew member, each dinghy, and the vessel as well! Sounds like a great income-producer! However, Mexico has promised to revamp and streamline their Pesca licensing procedures soon.

Radio Licenses

Carry a copy of all personal and ship's radio licenses and keep them with your important papers. Carry a copy of your ham operator's license, too. VHF radio licenses are no longer required by the FCC for recreational boats less than 65 feet in length and operating in U.S. waters. However, those planning to sail in foreign waters are required, under international rules, to be licensed for single side band radios and for Inmarsat satellite equipment. Applications for these licenses will continue to be processed by the FCC. Use form FCC753 or call the FCC at 800-322-1117.

Pet Papers

If you travel with pets, you must have with you all the health and inoculation papers relating to each animal. Some countries are very strict in this regard, and a few will not let your pet ashore until after a suitable quarantine period, if then. Most veterinarians can supply an *International Health Certificate* for your pet. They will examine your animal and certify it to be in good health by the issuance of the certificate. The routine examination and issuance of the certificate should cost less than $50. At that time, you should update your pet's rabies vaccination—which is required internationally. It should not be more than one year old. While you're at it, get boosters for distemper, bordatello, and carona virus—although these are not internationally required. After you return from cruising, you should get your pet checked for parasites, particularly if you've spent time in the third world.

Contact the U.S. Department of Agriculture, Veterinarian Services at 916-857-6170 for the specific requirements for each country you might want to visit. Health requirements relating to pets can vary from country to country. Additionally, you can contact the consulates of the countries you plan to visit for their current regulations before you leave the States, although this information should be available from the Veterinarian Services number above. Your final step should be to have your pet's International Health Certificate endorsed by the office of Veterinarian Services. They charge $16.50 for this service. This endorsement shows that a U.S. governmental agency verifies the authenticity of the document. Some South American countries will require this endorsement.

Insurance Papers

If your boat is insured, take along your boat's insurance policy and related papers. If you have property at home and carry a homeowner's or business umbrella policy that protects your liability, take that too. I have heard of cruisers being asked to show proof of insurance, though I believe this is still quite rare. If you are cruising uninsured, you might have to leave a marina or shipyard that requires proof of insurance. In an emergency, you could try to get temporary local insurance to comply with the requirement.

Copies of Ship's Papers

Make multiple copies of all important papers. Officials often ask for copies of certain documents for their records, and they never seem to have a copy machine in their office. So if you don't have copies available, you will have to wander around a strange town looking for a Xerox machine.

Creative Documents

Occasionally, you may encounter an unreasonable bureaucrat who tries his best to be demanding and difficult. There can be times, if you cruise long enough, when the ability to create an official-looking document aboard your boat would come in handy. With a computer, onion skin paper, a few stick-on gold seals of various sizes, and perhaps a small manual imprint embosser, you can create masterful-looking documents for unreasonable officials. It may not matter very much what it says. If it looks official enough, it might just do the job.

Pre-Cruise Medical Procedures

Seasickness

Every boat should have an array of techniques and medicines to offset this problem. If your crew hasn't been aboard a small boat in a seaway before, you should experiment in actual conditions to determine in advance what drugs will mediate or solve this near-totally-preventable illness. Just one severe bout with seasickness may be enough to cloud the cruising horizons for an otherwise agreeable sailing partner. You may have to try several prescriptions before you find the one that works best.

On our boat, Anna has to wear a scopolamine patch (72-hour protection) behind her ear the night before departure in order to get relief the following day. Depending on weather conditions, she might: 1) continue to wear the patch a second day, 2) cut it in half (not recommended by doctors for fear it may leak—but never did), 3) switch to Stugeron for the balance of the passage, or 4) stop the medication entirely if the passage were smooth. If her mouth became dry or her vision blurry, she immediately removed the scopolamine patch and substituted a less potent remedy. Other drugs, like Dramamine, Bonine, Marazine, and Antivert can also be tried. Carry Compazine suppositories in case nothing will stay in the stomach.

The manufacturer of Transderm-Scop (Scopolamine) patches (CIBA Consumer Pharmaceuticals of Woodbridge, N. J. 1-800 452-0051) has temporarily interrupted production. They claim patches should be available again sometime in 1997. Until the patches are back in production, you can still get scopolamine in gel form from certain compounding pharmacies. One dose of the gel rubbed in on the inside of the wrist will work for eight to 12 hours. Try Costa Mesa Pharmacy in Costa Mesa, CA at 714-642-0106 or Panorama Pharmacy in Los Angeles at 800-247-9767. Stugeron is a British medication and not available in the U.S. It is available in many Central and South American (or British Commonwealth) countries.

If you would like to try natural products, I have had good reports on an herbal extract made from ginger root, fennel seed, anise seed, and four other herbs. It is mixed with hot or cold water and is taken three to four times a day. Eight ounces sells for $65 and is good for 14 days of continuous exposure. The extract lasts a long time without refrigeration. Call The Herbal Spirit in Santa Barbara, CA at 805-962-9921. They will ship.

Vaccinations/Inoculations

Before departure, check with your county health department concerning their recommended shots for the countries you're planning to visit. Immunization shots can sometimes be given to crew members at local county health facilities. The immunizations that might require your attention would be: typhoid, yellow fever, tetanus/diphtheria, pneumococcal, meningococcal, hepatitis A and B, cholera, and polio. Be sure to check with your family doctor before proceeding with any pre-trip medical program.

Medical Records

If you have on-going medical problems, take copies of all your medical records and any x-rays that might be helpful in obtaining treatment in foreign countries.

Prescriptions—Visual and Medical

Keep copies of prescriptions for important drugs in your boat's medical kit, especially any medications with narcotics that could arouse suspicion in an onboard inspection. Also get a copy of your eyeglass prescription, just in case they go overboard. If you have this, you can get glasses replaced just about anywhere. In many Central and South American countries, medicines and drugs can often be purchased over the counter without a prescription and at bargain prices. See Chapter 8, ***Reference*** section for a listing of the **Medical Kit—Contents.**

Fish Poisoning

Exercise care when eating fish—fresh caught or while dining in restaurants. Fish poisoning is not uncommon in tropical areas and can be contracted through the fish you catch, buy, or eat ashore. See Chapter 7 - ***Tropic Travel Tips*****—Poisonous Fish and Critters.**

Medical Considerations for Crew Members

Skippers taking on non-family crew members should be particularly mindful of the potential medical problems coming aboard. You should be convinced that any chronic illnesses are controlled and that any needed medication is in their possession before you accept them as crew. Their medicines should be added to the ship's medical locker. Your crew should be asked to provide a doctor's prescription for each required medication. (This will be important when your vessel is inspected by a medical officer). A recurring illness or emergency can be a major disruption of your cruising plans and, perhaps, your itinerary.

In many foreign countries, the skipper is responsible for his crew—even for their airfare home if that is required. For this reason, many skippers with non-family crew members retain all passports in their possession until the voyage is completed. If your crew leaves the boat for any reason, your boat's departure will be delayed. You will not be cleared to leave port until all crew members are properly accounted for.

The Shakedown Cruise

In the rush to depart, the shakedown cruise is frequently relegated to the "if we have time we'll try to squeeze it in" category. This most-important step should be an integral part of your departure plans. Shortly before your planned leaving, schedule a short—but serious—local cruise to find the weak links in your cruising armor. Commercial and naval vessels never omit this vital step and for good reason. Tradition has shown that all elements in the ship's operation must be thoroughly tested and shaken down before it starts a voyage.

All your equipment and onboard cruising systems must be tested. The crew should be checked out on every piece of equipment. Put the boat under sail and really go somewhere. Don't just head for the nearest marina up the coast. Head right off shore and actually stand watches in a realistic trial of boat and crew. Navigate, stand watches, and cook underway. Spend several days learning what works and what doesn't. Learn what problems you have before departure. Practice reefing and heaving-to. Put up all the sails, pole out the jib downwind, and set the cruising chute. Try the autopilot and the watermaker. Learn to use the wind vane if you have one, and practice collecting the weather from your radio or fax.

When your shakedown is completed, head back to your home port armed with the list of problems to correct. Alterations and changes can be made at your home port more quickly and more cheaply than anywhere else. And while you're making those last minute corrections, think how potentially serious it might have been if any of these problems had occurred off shore at the beginning of the voyage. This single step of shaking down the boat and your crew before you leave will pay rich dividends in safer and more enjoyable cruising.

Chapter 6

Offshore And Underway

Ready for a long night,
Passage heads off shore.

Radio Communications

Once offshore, the ship's radios and e-mail computer links become the only source of information for those aboard. Each crew member needs to know how to operate the ship's radios. If the boat is amateur (ham) radio equipped, only the licensed operator is allowed to transmit over the air in normal use, even though anyone can receive. In an emergency, though, licensing would not be required. Therefore, every crew member needs to know how to operate all the radios onboard and be prepared to make distress calls should they be necessary. While underway or at anchor, it is good practice to have your radios pre-tuned to emergency channels or frequencies. Then, all that is necessary is to turn on the radio, in order to communicate with other boats, the USCG, or marine nets ashore. This simple procedure empowers every crew member with the ability to communicate with those capable of providing assistance in emergencies.

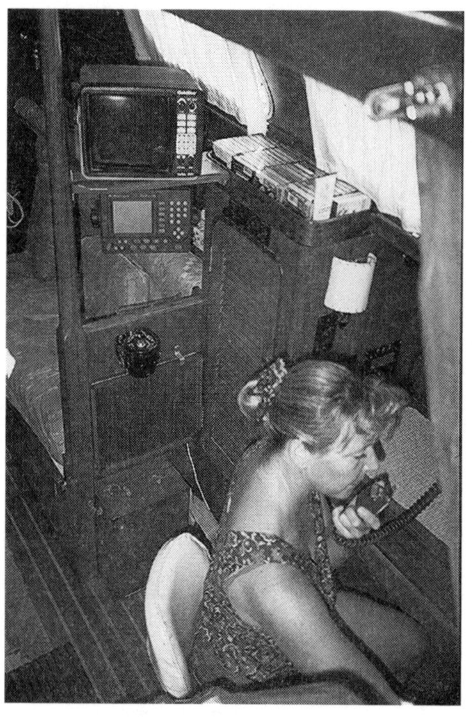

"I love this radio," says Anna. Note that radar and GPS are visible from the cockpit.

Federal rules prohibit the use of one radio for transmission on both ham and SSB frequencies. However, some newer SSB radios have this capability built in (anticipating a change of rules?), and older radios can be easily modified to provide both services. In an emergency, any crew member is allowed to transmit distress messages. Many cruisers use a radio that has been modified to provide this multiple coverage for emergency use. It is never unlawful to monitor (listen to) any frequency with whatever radio you have on board. See Chapter 5, ***Departure Countdown*—Staying In Touch** for more information.

Offshore Radio Services

Be it marine SSB or ham radio, each transceiver can provide the mariner with weather broadcasts, ship-to-shore communication, ship-to-ship communication, and (via marine nets) local cruising information. But, it will be up to you to determine the time and frequencies of these broadcasts. Some transmitted information will come from government agencies broadcasting WX and storm or hurricane warnings; some will come via informal, private radio groups called nets.

Services that allow you to "call home" with your marine radio are provided for a fee of $5 per minute by AT&T high seas operators. To use this service, it is best to establish your marine account with AT&T before departure. Otherwise, you will have to give your credit card number out over the air—not a good idea. Call 800-SEA CALL to register or request the fingertip guide to AT&T High Seas Radiotelephone Service. The pamphlet will explain what you need to get started and how to use this service.

AT&T's new service High Seas Direct (800-392-2067), drops phone charges to just $1.29 per minute, provides privacy with voice scrambling, but requires about $1000 of additional equipment for the boat—a hand set, with built-in keypad and digital display. This service does not provide e-mail. See Chapter 4, ***Outfitting Your Vessel for Cruising*** - **Electronics and Communications** for more.

Similar services to the above are available from individual land-based ham radio operators offering to "patch you through" to a stateside number. These "patches" are provided to you without cost if you are a licensed ham operator. Such calls are often available through marine radio nets as well as by individual ham operators. They are provided by shore-based hams who have special equipment to "patch" you into regular phone lines. The person you are calling is responsible for paying any long-distance charges from the shore-based ham operator to their own number.

Once underway, you will most likely start listening to various nets to learn the radio protocols, check-in procedures, and the services each net provides. Marine nets are organized with a "net control." This is the person who runs the net, allowing boaters to "check in," request information, or contact other boats. Anyone can listen to marine SSB and ham nets, but you must hold an amateur radio license to participate (transmit) on ham bands (frequencies). For any radio communication, you will first need to learn the necessary radio procedures. Communications from off shore can be lots of fun and open new doors in your cruising world. Gather radio information regarding nets and schedules before departure. See also Chapter 5, ***Staying In Touch.***

Passagemaking—Watch-keeping

When underway for more than just a few hours, you will need to establish some kind of a watch schedule. Without this onboard organization, you and your crew will not get sufficient rest to stay alert. This can lead to irritability and even accidents. Traditional watches were 4-hours long. But many cruising couples find this is too long to stand individual watches, so they try other options, such as three hours or even less. You need only find a system that works on your boat. Some crews maintain the watch schedule 24 hours a day. Others stand watches only at night. Occasionally, skippers try to do extra duty to spare their mates the night watches. This should be done only on very short passages or when the first mate cannot, for some reason, stand his or her own watch. Otherwise, the skipper will become exhausted from lack of sleep and could be unreliable in emergency situations.

For short 1- or 2-night passages, any watch system you try may seem awkward. Fatigue and lack of sleep are common problems on shorter passages. You will be glad to see the next landfall, get the anchor down, and get some rest. On longer passages, you will fall into a rhythm that allows each crew member adequate rest. Try various systems until you find one that works on your boat.

On our boat we often stood 1-hour watches on short (24-hour) overnight coastal passages. This worked for us, but I don't know anyone else who used it. The next day at anchor we usually took a long nap. I thought this arrangement kept both crew members "at the ready"—each person always quickly available without having to rouse from deep sleep when sailing close to shore—the area of most marine traffic and underwater hazards.

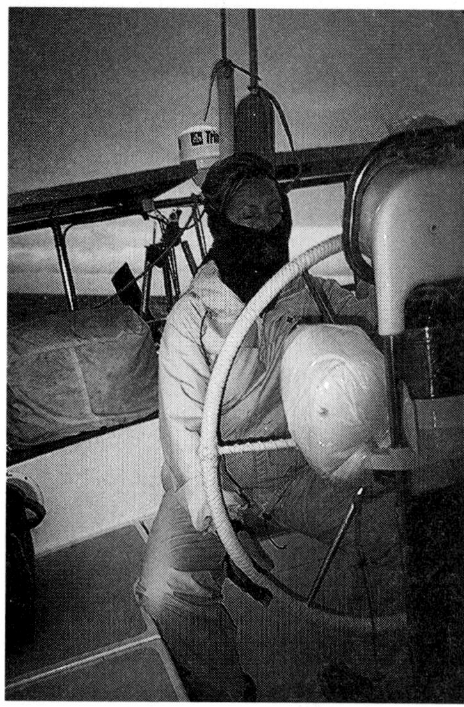

Stay in the tropics, so you'll never have to look like this.

Many cruisers say they do not like overnight passages. It violates no nautical law to say you love cruising, but hate standing night watches. That's the sentiment of lots of boaters. But whenever you're underway, watches must be stood, and crews must stay alert to protect the vessel and the people below. Maritime law requires someone to be on watch if the boat is underway.

For 2-person crews, you will need at least one good sea berth. It should be situated about amidships, or further aft. Berths in the forepeak will become unsuitable for sleeping in heavy weather. If you have a good sea berth on each side of the boat, you can be comfortable on either tack. Bunks should be equipped with lee cloths to hold you in your berth, even if the sea should try to roll you out. If possible, set up the bunk so that the person off watch can see into the cockpit—to check on what's going on up there. It is reassuring to know your partner is near at hand should they be needed.

Onboard Relationships

Frequently overlooked in the cruiser preparation process are the interpersonal relationships that are essential to a successful cruise. Fresh from their busy lifestyles and hectic preparations, the often exhausted crew jumps aboard at departure without thoughts as to the dramatic changes this new lifestyle requires.

At home the couple has had long-established patterns that have sustained their relationship. Cruising will test this relationship. Ashore, "she" has done this and been responsible for that, while "he" can be counted on to do this and supply that. But at sea and while cruising, these basic patterns must be changed to address the altered conditions of the cruising lifestyle.

While underway, there will be need for more teamwork—especially in situations like anchoring, reefing sails, docking, and maintenance projects. For better or worse, there will be more togetherness. Many activities, both aboard and ashore, will be shared with your partner. Aboard, you or your mate will be working in less-familiar situations, so stress is a likely by-product. On a small boat, tensions can easily develop and must be resolved to avoid frustration and conflict. I have a friend who jokes about "water soluble" cruising relationships—and there's probably lots of truth to that. Relationships can be severely challenged while living the cruising life within the confines of a small boat.

Each person must be willing to make concessions and adjustments to his and her new life aboard—particularly when underway. They must be willing to do and try things they would not usually do ashore. A lady friend of ours was able to diagnose and fix the diesel engine aboard their boat by carefully studying the engine manual. Discuss frankly and honestly your fears and concerns relating to all aspects of passagemaking. Whether at sea or ashore, cruising couples working together can achieve a closeness and camaraderie they seldom had at home.

Couple Relationships Underway

Basically, the cruising experience can be divided into two parts. The first part would be the actual underway portion of the cruise (only about 10% of the time), and the second part (about 90% of the time) would include everything else—the living aboard part plus all the things you do ashore. The major differences while you're voyaging will be such things as increased time together, increased

Toasting the voyage, a high point for every cruising couple.

closeness, and a lot more reliance on each other's developing boating skills and expertise.

Underway, someone must serve as captain. Generally this position defaults to the man, but not always. The vessel's captain should be the most experienced and competent sailor/sea person on board. In cases where both partners are equally skilled, I have heard of crews who alternate captains on a daily or weekly basis. On some boats there is almost no distinction between captain and first mate. There is shared responsibility for seamanship, navigation, and galley duty. This is probably the very best and most harmonious way to run a small boat.

Each boat's crew must work together to achieve a cruising relationship that fits their temperaments and personalities in this new cruising lifestyle. At the beginning of the cruise especially, fears, anxieties, and insecurities may alter your relationship with your mate from what it was before departure. Don't let this altered relationship torpedo your adventure. Frankly and honestly discuss your concerns and hesitations with your partner.

Both skipper and mate may have left highly competent positions in their prior employment experiences. They will each have to yield, change, and adjust to their new relationship underway. Each crew member may be required to do things afloat, like fix the head or bleed the fuel system—jobs that they might have hired out at their home marina. One of our friends calls cruising the place where you learn to *"do it yourself and slave."* In a recent article, a skipper said that cruising is "five percent sailing and 95 percent fixing things."

Each crew member must learn new skills and be prepared for situations not encountered at home. This fact is significant, since neither partner may be accustomed yet to the need for constant monitoring of engine, hull, rigging, and multiple boat systems. This will require increased effort devoted to maintenance and repair, and increased time to supply and re-provision the boat. For both crew members, the involvement with the basics of living aboard will be well beyond similar responsibilities in previous shore-based lifestyles.

While you're underway or maneuvering, decisions must frequently be made quickly without discussion or consensus. On occasions when there is time, the situation can be discussed—and decisions jointly made. When decisions are made by the skipper, they must be carried out immediately with good humor and without delay or argument. This last situation is an area that is not generally encountered while living ashore, and it may lead to misunderstandings with the first mate. The captain must not be too "militaristic" here—or else he or she could risk a mutiny. No one likes taking orders, particularly from their spouse. If the skipper becomes a Captain Bligh, the cruising dream can become a nightmare.

Let tact and reasonable volume levels prevail aboard. Keep in mind that raising your voice usually indicates your own insecurity and does nothing to ensure a faster response from your crew. Remember, too, that your "command authority" lasts only until the next anchorage, and then you will lose your "commission" and probably your dinner, too! Captains can only command when the boat is underway—just 10% of the time! For the remaining 90% of the time, the situation returns to a more shore-based relationship.

Women's Concerns - by Anna Gleckler

Many women learn to be good sailors and enjoy day sailing, racing, or short-distance coastal cruising. But with only a few exceptions, the idea of long-distance cruising is generally a man's dream. Yes, there are a few exceptions, but very few. During our 5-year cruise, I met several women single-handers and one man/women team where the woman was the skipper. There are exceptions, too, to the nesting syndrome—some women do seek as much risk and adventure as their men. But most don't.

While men tend to be seekers of risk and adventure, we women tend to seek safety and a comfortable nest. The idea of leaving home for an extended period of time to go voyaging on a small boat presents many concerns for women. Some of the pre-cruise concerns I felt were also expressed to me by other women planning to cruise or already underway. These concerns were about leaving family and friends, the loss of our homes, threatening storms, isolation, fear, confinement, boredom, a feeling of incompetence, loss of self-identity, feminine hygiene concerns, lack of confidence in our mate's abilities, and—perhaps most importantly—concerns about whether cruising would affect the relationship we had with our mates.

Cruising couples should learn to perform each other's cruising roles for possible emergencies, and to ease the anxiety of participation in activities not fully understood. Increased competence in nautical skills will go a long way in allaying the fears many women have when first venturing off shore.

For most women, there is a lot to worry about. But I quickly learned once we were underway, that with the right preparations, my pre-cruise concerns were replaced with positive experiences. It is important for women to find and focus on new hobbies and skills that will help them develop a new independence and identity from the one they had ashore. Most of my pre-cruise concerns quickly faded and eventually disappeared. For example, the absence of old friends was replaced quickly with a new fraternity of cruising women. My fears of isolation were soothed by daily radio contacts and various new hobbies, such as snorkeling, writing, and language study.

Boats are referred to as "she" for a good reason. Like a woman, boats require lots of tender loving care and take most of a man's time and money. Cruising, however, is also like a woman. It offers a man a kind of excitement with an element of risk and exploration. Boats can take men to sea, but when accompanied by their women, the voyage can be a lasting and memorable achievement for both partners.

Rules of the Road

Nautical Rules of the Road - The Inland and International Nautical Rules of the Road are the rules of marine right-of-way that apply to all vessels. These are much more than a courtesy code for boats passing, crossing, or overtaking one another. They are the legally-binding Inland and International Rules of the Road. The inland rules apply to all ships sailing U.S. inland waters, and the international rules affect all vessels anywhere on the high seas. Their intent is to prevent marine accidents, and to govern the responses one makes to marine traffic situations. They regulate the lights that ships show at night and the sounds they make in the fog. They determine which vessel has the right-of-way and what maneuvers each must take to avoid accidents. Each crew member should be familiar with these essential rules which are designed to prevent accidents and save lives. When you're on watch, these rules are part of the nautical bible that must be understood and obeyed. These rules apply to *all* vessels at sea—not just to large ships.

The U.S. Coast Guard publishes a handy pamphlet with the Rules of the Road and other pertinent information. It is available without charge at most marine stores or through U.S. Coast Guard Auxiliary offices everywhere. Call USCG for information at 800-368-5647 for the inland rules, or 202-

512-1800 for international rules of the road. A copy of the International Rules of the Road will cost you $8.00. *Chapman Piloting and Small Boat Handling* also contains copies of the Rules of the Road and Nautical Lights. Buy this from any marine store—it's an excellent reference book.

Cruising Protocols

Whatever hobbies people involve themselves in, it is generally required that they learn certain basic rules of behavior for that activity. Whether it's playing bridge, tennis, golf, or attending the theater, there are things expected of those who participate. That is certainly true in boating. Nautical traditions are old and honored, and ignorance of them can quickly paint the mariner as a novice or worse. Read on to avoid offending your new cruising friends:

Anchoring

Where and how to anchor when other boats are already in the anchorage area can be a difficult decision for the new cruiser. If there's one thing more than any other that gets cruisers uptight, it's anchoring procedures. Whether you're trying to get your own anchor or anchors down in a crowded anchorage with everyone staring at you, or you are defending what you feel is your territory from an anchoring interloper, an otherwise peaceful spot can sometimes turn testy. It's great sport at cocktail time to watch arriving boats go through their anchoring drills. Quiet anchorages can turn into arenas where shrill commands ring from bow to stern, and they echo across the bay during attempts at setting the hook.

Often, you can learn as much about what not to do, as well as what to do, just by watching these twilight arrivals. Your developing anchoring skills, honed through practice and observation, should lead to a growing confidence in this less-than-perfect art form. But we all get befuddled occasionally. So be prepared to laugh at yourself now and then, when you have one of those royal anchoring snafus. Just keep observing the best anchorers, and borrow from their techniques until you're comfortable and confident in your own anchoring skills. See Chapter 8, ***Reference*** for recommended anchoring procedures and **Quiet Anchoring** hand signals.

Flag Display

National flags, courtesy flags, and burgees are often displayed aboard cruising boats incorrectly. Flag etiquette is a bit like the nautical Rules of the Road—not considered really essential material by some boaters. Flag etiquette was established by long tradition, but it does not carry the same legal weight as the rules governing maritime traffic.

However, flag traditions do display (for all to see) the mariner's knowledge and expertise in these matters. Correctly flying flags shows your awareness of the marine heritage you're involved in. It shows your respect for your own country, as well as for the countries you are visiting. On one occasion in the Dominican Republic, I was informed by the Port Captain that the blue in our courtesy flag was not the proper shade. On another occasion in Trinidad, we were informed by a passing naval patrol boat that we were flying their ensign upside down, causing me a red face indeed! Others do notice and care about how their country's flag is displayed.

The proper display, placement, and size of the flags flown on your boat will do much to identify you as a knowledgeable cruiser and keep you out of trouble with local harbor masters and patrol boats from the country you're visiting. There is an excellent small book called *Guide to Flags of the World* (available at most marine stores) that you will find most helpful to have aboard. See Chapter 8, ***Reference*—Flag Etiquette** for flag display information.

Dinghy Usage

The fast inflatable dinghy is a boon to the cruising sailor. But it also carries a responsibility in anchorages shared with other boats. Be especially mindful of swimmers and snorkelers while you're at anchor. Throttle back and reduce speed, noise, and wake when you are in close proximity to other boats. They will probably do the same for you during your afternoon siesta.

When visiting other boats, ask the skipper where he wants you to tie your dinghy to avoid boarding ladders, wind vanes, etc. Streaming the dinghy aft is generally the best spot to avoid problems. If your dinghy marks or scrapes hulls, or if it needs fenders, then inform the other skipper and help secure your dinghy to avoid these problems.

If you are tying your dinghy to a dock with lots of other dinghies, leave five to 10 -extra feet on your painter. This allows late-comers to move your boat aside and still get to the dock to unload. See Chapter 8, ***Reference*—Dinghy Accessories.**

Noise

In a lovely and quiet anchorage, it doesn't take much noise to be obtrusive. The biggest culprits here are the generators that many cruisers—both power and sail—require for their lifestyle afloat. Particularly bad are the large units that create noise and fumes that others in the anchorage must endure. Those little noisy units that some sailboats start up on the foredeck are just as bad. Arrange your charging hours for the middle of the day, when the noise would be less bothersome and the wind can blow away the fumes. If you use a generator, drop your hook where others aren't subject to your disturbance.

Finally, consider the cruising lifestyle you've gone cruising to achieve. Is it really better with all those electrical accessories that require you to turn your boat into a floating power plant? After all, if you've gone cruising to find a new freedom, to rediscover simple pleasures, and to escape the rat race—why insist on bringing all the complexities of your shore life with you? Most of those creature-comfort gadgets (beyond the necessary modern equipment to safely cruise your boat) will require lots of attention, maintenance, and electricity. Don't become a slave to your boat's equipment and miss the very reasons you chose to go cruising.

Lots of pot lucks -- if you want them.

Potlucks, Sundowners, & Beach Parties

The cruising scene is highly social—if you want it to be. There will be many opportunities to meet others, party, and make good friends. The easiest way to tarnish your social image is to show up for cruiser gatherings without your fair share of beer, ice, drinks, food, or hors d'oeuvres. While cruising, every boat must be self-contained—onboard supplies are not replaceable until the next supply port, if then. Provision your own boat in anticipation of these special social events and the possible increase of entertainment needs.

If you're ashore and meeting other cruisers on the beach for sundowners and snacks, meet and assist the arriving dinghies as they come up to the beach. It will win you lots of brownie points. Exiting from a moving dinghy in the surf with food in your hands can lead to wet arrivals and loss of goodies. Besides, standing on the beach sipping your drink and giggling—while others are having a hard time getting ashore—is a sure way to set yourself up for when it happens to you—as it certainly will.

Assistance

Most cruisers at some point in their voyaging will need the help of others to avoid potentially dangerous situations or to solve troublesome equipment problems. Maybe your mechanical or electrical skills could save the day for a boat in distress. Maybe you could assist in towing or helping a boat that has gone aground. Perhaps others could benefit from your local knowledge of an anchorage you just left—such as how to handle a troublesome harbor master, problems of dinghy thievery, or just a great diving spot you discovered. Perhaps you could share information on a wonderful local experience or land trip at the anchorage they're headed for. Whatever the situation, your willingness to help could literally be a lifesaver for a fellow cruiser. Yachties comprise a small and close-knit fraternity—and, as Anna says, "What goes around, comes around."

Cruise Termination—Causes of Failure

The majority of causes leading to cruise termination are people problems. Relatively few cruise failures relate to the vessel or its equipment. The following list might help to identify the potential problem areas and help you personally prepare for your coming change in lifestyle.

Crew incompatibility. Getting along on a boat requires different skills and adjustments than when ashore. If you can, sail extensively together and/or live together on a boat before committing time and money to a long cruise. Be very careful of taking on additional crew members for a passage unless you know them well and have sailed together before. Good friends ashore don't necessarily or automatically turn into good crew members when exposed to the occasional rigors, stress, and discomfort of cruising.

No experience in cruising. The crew is not ready for offshore and underway situations. All the pre-cruise time was devoted to preparing the vessel. There were few actual sailing experiences to prepare the crew for voyaging and life afloat. Skippers must schedule necessary sea time for practice and training. This single requirement can do much to reduce stress and increase comfort levels aboard.

Medical problems. Any chronic medical problem or emergency could abruptly terminate the voyage. Even first-passage seasickness is enough, sometimes, to cause a total and permanent change of heart. Insist on a thorough medical checkup for each crew member. Test seasickness remedies on short practice cruises before the big departure.

Lack of physical conditioning. Departing with a soft and flabby crew, conditioned only at an office desk, is a poor way to start your cruising dream. Occasional physical demands could require you and your crew's maximum efforts. Poor physical conditioning can lead to discomfort and accidents. Get in shape before casting off.

Skills in sailing and seamanship are not sufficient for the situation. You could be lucky and learn underway, but a rough first passage could easily end the cruise early. Good sailing and seamanship skills will lead to safer, faster, and more comfortable passages and a less stressed-out skipper and crew.

Equipment Failures. Although most cruise terminations relate to human problems, sometimes these conditions are brought on by equipment failures. These can tax your patience and endurance. Make sure your boat is in top cruising condition before departure. You don't need all the latest gear, but what equipment you do have should be maintained in first-class condition.

No shakedown cruise. The local shakedown cruise is designed to test the crew and vessel in a variety of situations. Find the problems and weaknesses in your boat and crew on your shakedown trip and fix them before departure. Practice procedures and gain confidence in your boat and yourselves. Your shakedown cruise should be much more than an afternoon sail. It should thoroughly test your boat and crew.

Fear. Some folks are overly fearful—especially about things relating to cruising on a boat. As you begin your cruising, it is common to have fears of possible scary situations you've heard about, but have not yet encountered. Heavy weather, overnight passages on dark nights, lightning storms, sailing out of sight of land, isolated anchorages, pirates, and traveling inland in the third world are just some of the possible scenarios. As you get more adventurous and accustomed to the cruising lifestyle, you will come to realize that you are probably much safer cruising than you would be at home in the U.S. Most cruisers find that these situations become commonplace and much less stressful. Be sure to give yourself time to adjust to these new cruising situations which are so unrelated to your previous shore-based existence. Learn how to perform all onboard tasks to boost your confidence in emergency situations.

Concerns at Home

Most folks out cruising remain committed to eventually returning home, or to some other shoreside location. Their cruising is not open-ended, but limited by time, employment, health, or finances. They have parents, children, jobs, or property at home. At some point they plan to resume their life ashore. Modern cruisers are fortunate that electronics and air travel have made keeping in touch much easier than ever before. There are many world-wide locations where you can safely leave your boat for a trip home. Your leave of absence from cruising can range from a few days to many months. In your cruising budget, allow for the eventuality of going home for occasional visits. It will greatly ease the stresses related to lingering land-based responsibilities. This approach can also serve to extend your cruising experience.

Controlling the Cruising Budget

There are many ways to hold down the cruising budget. To begin with, sail a small, simple, and uncomplicated boat. Less equipment and gear means less original cost and also less maintenance expense. Do your own boat work—many cruisers do all of their own maintenance. Some even build their own boats. Eat like the locals when in foreign countries. U.S. food products can be expensive abroad. Provision at the open public markets. When traveling ashore, use only public transportation. Restrict your eating ashore. Before leaving, frequent marine swap meets and garage sales for necessary marine equipment. Limit your electronics to the bare essentials. Learn the language of the countries you're visiting—so you can barter and trade with the locals for your cruising needs.

Navigation and Plotting Procedures

The use of electronics—such as radar and GPS—should not be used as an excuse to avoid usual navigation procedures. On every leg of a voyage, the navigator should establish a rhumb-line course

I need a bigger chart table!

to the destination. Plot this line with a soft pencil on a chart that shows both your departure and destination points. Above the course line, write the magnetic heading to your destination. Note hazards, water depths, possible obstructions, shoaling, and land masses that you will need to avoid. Periodically, at least every hour off shore and more frequently if coastal cruising, plot the position taken from your GPS along the rhumb line. Circle the dot marking your position, write down the time, and mark it as a "fix." If you are not on your rhumb line course, correct your heading now. It is not enough to simply know your latitude and longitude and assume you know where you are. You must always relate that to a current nautical chart to get the total picture.

When you're coastal cruising, if there is a charted and recognizable object ashore, occasionally take a bearing by sighting over the ship's compass or with a small hand-bearing compass. If you use your hand-bearing compass, stay away from any metal (like the shrouds) when taking the bearing. On most boats, this bearing line can be considered a magnetic bearing, and it can be plotted using the magnetic compass rose on the chart. Label the bearing line with the time and compass bearing. Extend the bearing line from the object shown on the chart to cross with your course line—to get a "most-probable position." Compare this with a "fix" from the GPS taken at the same time. The two positions should be reasonably close together. This is one way to double-check your plotting and to keep up your navigation skills at the same time.

If you're using electronic charts, be aware that dead batteries, electrical system failures, equipment breakdowns, or a lightning strike can wipe out all of your electronic navigation tools at once. These situations are not uncommon. Be prepared to back up each eventuality with traditional navigation procedures—like bearing-taking, regular position plotting, traditional charts, and sextant observations. Just in case, take an inexpensive plastic sextant, an "instant" navigation text, a quartz watch, and a celestial calculator for the tables and

almanac. If everything else fails, a highly motivated skipper can soon become a "traditional navigator" if need be.

Gathering Weather Information

Now that you're underway, it is up to you to gather all necessary weather (WX) information. WX data and forecasts can come from official sources such as the National Weather Service and U.S. Coast Guard broadcasts, or from informal marine nets and land-based amateur forecasters. It can also come from your own ship's instruments and from your on-site observations. Since many of the official sources of WX information require that you analyze and forecast their raw data and plot it on plotting sheets, some cruisers rely heavily on non-official sources that do the predictions and forecasts for you. Many of the amateur forecasters provide outstanding service for cruising sailors. Most marine nets (both SSB and ham) offer updated WX information each day. See Chapter 2, ***Preparing Yourself For Cruising*—Weather.**

Heavy Weather

There will be times when you will want to take action to ease the motion of the boat in the seaway and lessen the wear and tear on gear and crew—you just want to pull over to the side of the road and take a nap. In fact, there is a procedure that can be taken by small boats to achieve these goals.

Heaving-to (Sailboats)

Along with reefing techniques, heaving-to should be considered part of your first line of defense against wind, weather, and fatigue. It should be practiced during the shakedown cruise. Like reefing though, you shouldn't wait until you feel really threatened or begin to have equipment failures. Heaving-to is an easy method of controlling excessive motion of the boat and reducing strain on the rig. It gives an opportunity for the entire crew to get some needed rest. When properly hove-to, your boat should lie comfortably 30° to 60° to wind and sea without a person on the helm.

When you're caught in a blow, the motion of a boat hove-to is much more comfortable than when underway. It is also a useful technique to use when you arrive at a strange anchorage at night and don't want to enter until light. You won't want to sail back and forth off the entrance all night, so heave-to and relax until dawn. Some boats heave-to just to allow the cook to operate more comfortably below—not a bad idea if you want a good hot meal.

Dressed for heavy weather.
Note furled jenny and heavy-weather jib on break-away forestay.

Each boat behaves differently when hove-to. You must experiment with your own vessel until you are sure you have found the right sail combination to achieve the desired effect. Lots of boats use a combination of reefed main and partly furled jib. This may be just the sail combination you had up when you decided to heave-to, or you may want to reduce sail a bit more before your maneuver. In any case, all that is necessary is to haul the jib in tight and then slowly tack the boat. Don't pull the jib through, but let it catch the wind aback on the opposite tack. As the boat stops and settles down, experiment with the main. You want it to just fill, not flog. You don't want to lay abeam the swells where big seas could threaten the boat. Set your helm to bring the bow into the wind—the backed jib will balance this by setting the bow down. The boat's motion and forward progress is largely neutralized. With this rig your boat should lie comfortably with the wind forward of the beam. Lash or lock your wheel or tiller when you find the right combination.

The course of the boat over the bottom (fore-reaching) can be partially controlled by adjustments of the mainsail, but basically it will be more downwind than across the wind. Most boats will tend to drive slowly forward as they drift obliquely downwind.

If this sail combination doesn't seem to work on your boat, try using just a double- or triple-reefed main alone, pulled in tight. Some boats have good luck with this. If you have a ketch or yawl, try sail combinations using the mizzen. Just remember, you want the boat to lie to the wind without tacking, while reducing excessive rolling and motion. The keel slipping nearly sideways through the water will create a slick to windward that will have a leveling effect upon the seas.

Heaving-to (Powerboats)

Nordhavn 46 designed for offshore cruising handles this weather well.

If you're cruising on a powerboat, the procedure is similar. You want the bow of the boat positioned 30° to 60° into the seas to reduce strain and motion. You do not want to lay abeam the seas where the motion could be extreme or the boat could be rolled. If you're taking the seas on the starboard bow, experiment with power and helm to find the most comfortable settings. It may be that the autopilot will hold this position for you and allow you to rest. If your boat carries a mast, the steadying sail can be of real value in these conditions. If the weather worsens, reduce power so that you are just holding your position with no forward progress. If holding the bow to the seas becomes difficult, try using only the opposing prop (if you have twin screws). For example, if you are taking the seas on the starboard bow, try using only the port screw to hold your position.

When you can no longer hold the bow to the seas, you will have to turn your stern to the waves and run with them. Since the seas will be moving with you, to maintain steering control you may have to use engine power to move water past the rudder surface. If the boat is now moving too fast for safe control, to avoid broaching (burying the bow and turning abeam the seas) you will have to slow it down by trailing warps or deploying a sea anchor.

Maintenance Schedules

All of your marine gear will require frequent inspection and regular maintenance. Get organized and "exercise" all the mechanical, electrical, and electronic systems on a routine basis. Gear left unused for extended periods

What a great view, but don't rock the boat!

tends to fail quickly when cruising. Marine exposure, humidity, and lack of fresh water for wash downs takes its toll. Lubricate, grease, and inspect constantly. Use a magnifying glass on fittings, swages, and turnbuckles. Look for signs of failure such as broken wire strands in the rigging or hairline cracks in swages and turnbuckles. If you find any, replace them ASAP. *You did bring spares, didn't you?* Carry spare wire (long enough for the longest piece of standing rigging on board) and Sta-Lock or Norseman fittings to replace or repair any damaged rigging aboard your boat. With these fittings, you can easily make onboard repairs yourself with just a screwdriver and crescent wrench.

Go aloft before every significant passage for routine inspection of fittings, cotter pins, light bulbs, blocks and sheaves. Check your running rigging daily when you're underway. Because of the constant motion in a seaway, halyards and sheets can become badly chafed very quickly. As the old salts say, "freshen the nip;" reversing the sheets, halyards, and mooring lines can double their life.

Below in the engine room, the engine, transmission, and all mechanical and electrical equipment will require regular attention. "Out of sight, out of mind" is all too true, to your great detriment. Attention to batteries, belts, filters, impellers, pumps, and oil changes will prevent many a problem. Hoses, hose clamps, seacocks, and water leaks are other things to check for in your maintenance schedule. Some skippers have regular check-off lists to assist them and to avoid overlooking important items in their maintenance routines—an excellent idea.

Bottom Cleaning

When you're cruising in remote areas—and especially in the tropics—you will have to be able to maintain a clean boat bottom. Your boat will power more efficiently and sail better if you do. Many cruisers do their own bottom cleaning either by free-diving (without a scuba tank) or by using scuba tanks.

In fact, there may be no other way to get the job done when you are on an extended cruise and far from major cruising highways. If no one on board can do it, you may be able to find a native to do it for you. They will have to free-dive to do the job, but many natives are used to diving for lobster, clams, and seafood, and have developed good staying power underwater.

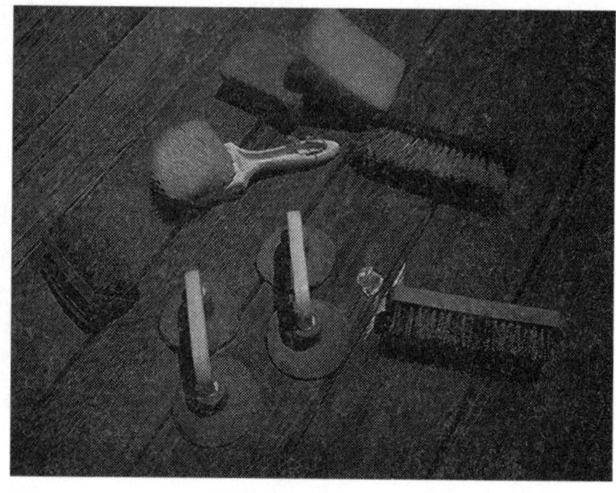

You'll need all these to keep your bottom clean.

For the hull, you will need a large sponge, rough terry cloth rags, large medium and stiff scrub brushes, plus two sets of suction cups with handles so you can get some leverage underwater while scrubbing. For the prop, shaft, and strut, a large stiff putty-knife will come in handy. Use a flat screw driver to clean well up into the through-hulls. Carry plenty of spare zincs on board, so you can replace them whenever you're diving for fun or cleaning the bottom.

If you are prepared and can do your own maintenance, you can probably avoid shipyards for a considerable length of time—maybe multiple years if you start off with a heavy coat of scrubable bottom paint. Incidentally, we found third-world bottom paint to be very good. It's not necessary to take your own, although there may be places where special paints will be hard or impossible to find.

Ugh, I'll be glad when this bottom job is over.

Cooking Underway

Baking in the tropics.

Cooking under sail (or power) in a seaway can be trying and not without some risk. You need a gimbaled stove free to swing with the motion of the boat. It should have fiddle rails, and pot holders on the burners to keep the pans secure while being used underway. You also need a safe place for the cook to operate; one that's secure and out of the traffic pattern. On many short passages, having pre-planned menus can reduce the need to cook underway—or eliminate it. On longer passages, you'll need to prepare hot food and meals in the galley. For rough conditions, have backup menus that minimize stove use.

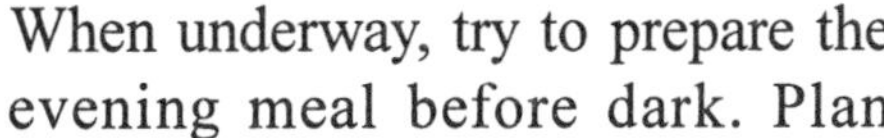

When underway, try to prepare the evening meal before dark. Plan simple menus that use pre-packaged or canned meals. For night watches, put hot water in thermos jugs or hot pots, so the on-watch crew can have instant beverages and soups without using the stove. When underway, put snacks and finger foods in sealed Tupperware containers within easy reach from topside. Forethought on these matters can make for a happy on-watch crew and better sleeping for those off watch. It's not fun to be in your bunk, trying to get some sleep, and have someone rummaging through the galley looking for coffee or snacks when they should be topside and alert.

By the way, your below-deck lighting system should include adequate red (or blue/green) night lights to allow the on-watch crew safe and quiet access to the interior—yet not destroy their night vision.

The cook must always be aware of the danger of burns. In the tropics, do not cook in your bathing suit. Wear a protective apron, slip on a pair of shoes, and make sure you use a galley safety belt if your galley layout requires it when underway.

Non-skid ("Sure Grip") rubberized strip matting from West Marine and Boat/U.S. stores will keep most things from sliding about the galley, but hot food and pans must always be placed in your deep sinks to minimize spills and prevent disasters. Make sure your gimbaled stove swings properly and has fiddle rails that keep your pots and pans in place on the stove top. Use rubberized matting on the table too, and things will tend to stay in their places. On your dinnerware, run a bead of clear silicon seal around the bottom, and set the dishes (silicon down) on a piece of wax paper—to level the fresh silicon. When dry, you'll have non-skid cups and tableware that will stay put.

Marine Emergencies

Happily, onboard cruising accidents are not frequent—but they are not uncommon. Muscle injuries, strains, and lacerations (perhaps in that order) are the things to avoid. In rough weather, falls on deck, across the cockpit, down the companionway, or into an open hatch can be incapacitating, painful, and potentially serious. Pain killers, muscle relaxants, and large Ace-type bandages are *must* items in your medical kit. The injured person may have to continue to function, even in pain, until the boat is in a safe anchorage. Look out for the anchor windlass—it gobbles line, chain, and *fingers*. I've come close several times!

Head injuries are potentially more serious. Booms and spinnaker poles can be the culprits here. Review and rehearse all sail-handling procedures in calm weather before trying them in a seaway. Tense, tired, and sleepy crews do make mistakes. Practice your sail-handling procedures until they're automatic.

Man Overboard

For man-overboard situations, determine what method and what gear you will use to bring the person back aboard. This is not an easy task, particularly if the person has been injured or is suffering from hypothermia. The *LIFESLING*, available from West Marine (800-538-0775) for about $150, is a popular approach to retrieving a man overboard. It incorporates a horseshoe float that encircles the person in the water and is attached to the boat with a long line. A 3-part hoisting tackle is used to bring the person on board. This procedure must be practiced with the weakest member of the team doing the actual retrieval. Rear-access boarding ladders, as found on many modern reverse-transom boats, can be a big help here. The boarding ladder is permanently mounted at the transom waterline, making it much easier for the person in the water to help himself or herself back on board. Whatever method you use, it is important to think it through and rehearse for this eventuality. Each crew member must know how to respond in an emergency.

Some 2-person crews opt to trail a floating safety line aft whenever they're sailing off shore. It's a good idea and could save your life. Use a brightly-colored polypropylene line about 100 feet long. Polypropylene floats. Tie a loop (with a bowline) that's big enough to go under your arms, or use a small float at the end. If you should go overboard, you still have a good chance of catching the safety line that's floating astern. Be sure each crew member has a whistle around his or her neck when on watch—just in case all other crew members are sleeping.

Chapter 7

Tropic Travel Tips

(special considerations for tropical cruising)

Awnings—Sun Protection

Once you get into the tropics, the need for additional sun protection while anchored will be all too obvious. Try to get a partial or full-sun awning made for your boat before departure. This will take time to design and sew, and it will take a very knowledgeable and skilled canvas worker to build it. It should cover as much of the deck as possible (some include the foredeck too) and be designed to be used when at anchor. For underway cockpit sun protection, you need a Bimini top that protects the helmsman. Your sun awning should be able to withstand winds to 25 knots or so. Since you will need to take it down in stronger winds, the ability to drop it quickly or roll it up is a big advantage. Your sun awning can mount above other existing canvas, such

Full sun awning and aft Bimini.

as dodger, Bimini, or rain awning. Sun awnings can often make a difference of 10 degrees or more inside the boat.

This cockpit screening provides shade and air flow.

Ventilation and Screening

The importance of adequate ventilation while cruising in the tropics cannot be over emphasized. When you're anchored, opening-hatches overhead and opening-ports in the cabin sides will never be closed except for rain. Most boaters also rig wind scoops for the hatches over their bunks. Wind scoops are commercially available at most chandleries. In addition to the scoops, take 12-volt automotive-type fans for critical spaces such as the galley and sleeping areas. Install them after you have lived aboard awhile and have determined the best locations.

Anticipate the need for ventilation even when it's raining (in the tropics, that's often the case) or when you must close all the ports. Plan to rig a small waterproof rain awning over your forward hatch that keeps the water out but lets the air in. Take extra awning material and thread just for these situations. Once you're in hot climates, you can determine the best design by looking at other cruising boats.

Rain cover over foreward hatch allows air flow through the boat.

In some areas, screens on your

hatches and ports will be required in order to keep pests out of the boat. In some cases, the pests can be those tiny no-see-ums (sand flies) that can fly through regular screening. You will need to use fine-mesh screening available at stores specializing in camping and outdoor supplies. It's generally sold by the yard.

Clothing

Your clothing needs while cruising will depend a great deal on where you choose to sail. The intent of this book is to prepare you for cruising in mid-latitudes and especially the tropics—the areas where most cruisers head. For specialized high-latitude clothing, the mariner is well-advised to seek professional opinions and input from previous voyagers to those areas.

Even if you head for the tropics, each crew member will still need a set of good foul-weather gear, although we frequently stood watch in a bathing suit or shorts. But if it blew and rained hard enough, our foul-weather tops always felt good. But generally it stayed so warm that sometimes on calm night passages I would sneak a 2 a.m. beer.

We had just one rule regarding clothes that we always followed. That rule was that when underway the person on watch must always wear a pair of deck shoes to avoid accidents and injury. This rule obviously protects the toes and feet, but also improves the performance of the person working the foredeck.

In the tropics your clothing needs will drop to almost nothing—few clothes, rarely any shoes, and never any socks. Loose-fitting and light clothes (the less the better) are the only thing you can tolerate. Take a lot of swim suits, shorts, T-shirts, and thongs. You will also need extra hats and sun glasses. Plan on losing several hats and at least a couple pair of glasses over the side. Use only Polaroid glasses—use them for eyeball navigation and UV protection too. These glasses cut the glare on water and allow you to see below the surface—absolutely essential in coral reef areas.

For the infrequent times when cruisers need to look good, a man can take a pair or two of long pants and a couple short sleeved sport shirts—don't forget the socks. For the ladies, Anna says to take loose, thin, one-piece cotton dresses and a pair of nice sandals.

Bathing and Hygiene

On boats with a limited fresh-water supply, salt water bathing will save lots of water. If you do this over-the-side, it's a good way to cool down as well. After you're wet, suds up with Joy liquid soap on deck, then jump back in and rinse off. Joy soap sudses up well in salt water. If you don't like the idea of leaving salt on your body (although there's not much left after toweling), rinse again with about a quart of fresh water before drying off. That's all it takes to feel clean and fresh. Plastic Sun Showers hung on the foredeck work well. Some folks carry a pump-up garden sprayer for showering and say that also does the job. Lots of newer boats have permanent cockpit or stern platform showers for rinsing off with fresh water.

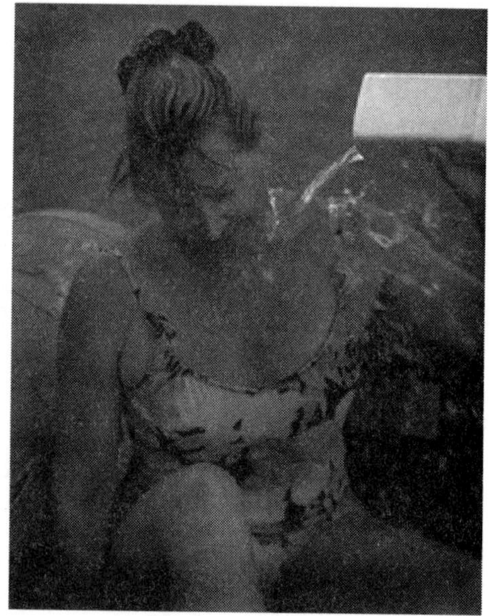

Dinghy bath with fresh water from a thunderstorm.

Tropical Health Considerations

Water and Parasites

You'll be drinking lots of sodas and beer in the tropics and not just because they taste good. The supply of potable drinking water can often be suspect. When ashore, be cautious of drinking water anywhere unless you can be sure of its purity. When eating out, don't trust the water or ice unless you can be convinced they're safe. The tinkle of ice in your soda may be all it takes to make you ill and cause diarrhea. You can generally trust canned or bottled beverages and hot coffee or tea, but not untreated water or ice. This is why you must always add chlorine bleach or iodine when refilling your water tanks.

If you're traveling inland, you must eat and drink ashore. In that case take tetracycline from the ship's medical kit. This antibiotic can be used prophylactically while you're on the trip to *prevent* illness (dose 250mg, twice a day). Tetracycline can cause hypersensitivity to the sun. (Doxcycline can also be used prophylactically. Dosage is 100mg, twice a day.) Take along some Imodium AD too, but this is helpful only after you get diarrhea. You should clear all this with your family doctor before departure.

No matter how careful you are, the tropics and the third world expose you to illnesses and parasites that can eventually enter your system and cause problems. A stool test is the only way to determine what ails you. Tests and treatment for parasitic problems are best conducted in the areas where these problems are frequently encountered. Local doctors there are used to seeing these kinds of medical conditions and readily understand how to treat them. Often the treatment is a 10-day regimen of Flagyl, but check with the medical professionals.

Medical Care Ashore

You'll find surprisingly good medical care available in many third world countries. However, it is often confined to cities and larger metropolitan areas and is not as widely available as in the States. A cruising doctor-friend had cataract surgery performed on both eyes while in Caracas, Venezuela. He was totally pleased and said he could not get this procedure in the U.S. Two women cruisers had hysterectomies performed in Cartagena, Colombia. They both thought they had excellent care. A crew member on my own boat had excellent care at a village infirmary in the Marquesas for fish (*ciguatera*) poisoning. The list goes on. Besides receiving good care, the patient also benefits from third world pricing which is much, much lower than in the U.S. By the way, most drug supplies are available over the counter—at substantial savings.

Poisonous Fish and Critters—ciguatera toxin

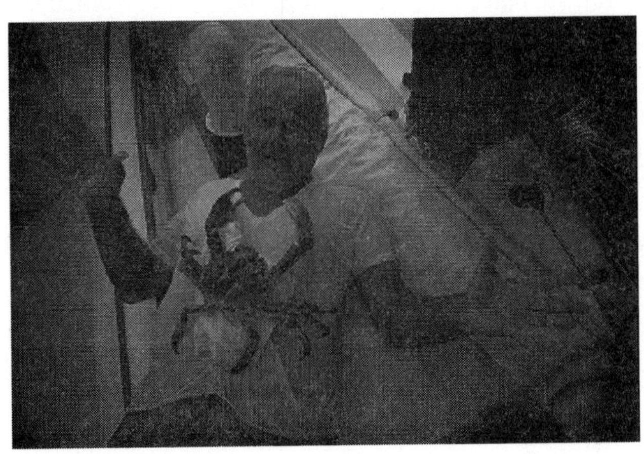

Crab attack!

While cruising in tropical waters you must be aware of poisonous sea life not usually encountered in more temperate climates. Fish, textile cone shells, jellyfish, and corals are all potentially poisonous or toxic. Any and all of these sometimes poisonous critters can cause mild to fatal poisoning and illness. In addition, you sometimes encounter stonefish, stingrays, toadfish, and the tiny (but poisonous) blue octopus in tide pools. These last two principally found in Australia. Learn which critters to avoid in the areas you're cruising.

Textile Cones appear in shallow water like bits of brown, yellow, and orange textile plaid cloth. These beautiful 2- to 3-inch shells, often found in the reef areas of the Indo-Pacific, have a tiny barbed spear that injects a potentially

Clam attack!

lethal poison (mortality rate of 20%). Do not handle or collect such shells.

Jellyfish have long strands of stinging cells that release toxins on hapless swimmers. There are several varieties, including the Portuguese man-of-war whose venom is similar to that of a cobra and nearly as potent. Intense stinging and burning may be the first indication that you're up close and personal with a jellyfish. They are nearly invisible, so their presence in the water can go undetected. Rubbing the skin with sand or a towel is not recommended, because it only triggers off un-discharged stinging cells. Prompt application of alcohol, gasoline, diesel fuel, vinegar, beer, or even urine helps to inactivate the toxin. This procedure is supposed to shrink the tentacles and allow them to be scraped off with a knife blade without furthering poisoning.

Tropical *corals* are razor sharp, and even minor scrapes and cuts can go weeks without healing. Bacterial infection due to a host of micro-organisms living on the reef is the problem. Promptly cleanse the wound by aggressively scrubbing it with hydrogen peroxide. Use a soft brush to remove all the fine particles still embedded in the wound. It'll hurt, but diluted chlorine bleach is also good on coral cuts to complete the cleaning process. Keep the wound clean and dry. If infection occurs, use a broad spectrum antibiotic like tetracycline, which can be taken orally or applied topically to the wound.

Avoid eating fish caught in the tropics (even in restaurants) without considering the possibility that they carry *ciguatera poisoning*. These poisons, found in many different species of fish, are not killed by boiling, cooking, or freezing. Outbreaks of fish poisoning occur randomly throughout the temperate, semi-tropic, and tropic areas of the globe. Though largely a tropical malady, ciguatera fish poisoning can occur anywhere between latitudes 35° North and 35° South. Florida, the Caribbean, French Polynesia, Hawaii, and Australia commonly have outbreaks of ciguatera fish poisoning.

Fish become poisonous when they eat microscopic organisms which attach themselves to marine algae. The algae grow on coral reefs in tropical or semitropical regions. The toxins get passed along the food chain from small plant-eating fish to larger fish, to predatory fish, and finally to man. Fish that are frequently poisonous are the snappers, barracuda, dorado, amberjack, grouper, and kingfish. There are many others, but these predacious fish are common carriers of ciguatera toxin. Fish that are poisonous one season may not be poisonous the next—or even at the next anchorage or island.

Outbreaks of ciguatera poisoning correspond to ecological damage to the reefs. Whether by storm, natural disasters, shipwreck, or underwater explosions, reef damage seems to cause the toxic organisms to swim freely and spread rapidly. This can cause an outbreak of fish poisoning.

The symptoms for ciguatera poisoning are numerous—from gastrointestinal to neurological to cardiovascular disorders. Initially, the symptoms are similar to severe food poisoning, but they last 14 to 21 days. Residual effects can last many months and in some cases are fatal. Onset of the illness generally comes within 1-2 hours of eating the infected fish, but it can start as much as 24 hours later in some cases.

On a cruise to the South Pacific, my own crew contracted fish poisoning twice within a period of one year. The first time, we were at anchor in the Tuamotus (Polynesia) and had feasted with the village chief on fish caught by his son—contradicting the adage about asking the locals which fish are safe to eat. We were very sick for several days, but within a week we were recovering. But for months after, whenever we dove into the water we felt a tingling, like "pins and needles" on the skin.

The second time, less than six months later, was in the Marquesas (Polynesia). The red snapper had been given to us by a fisherman (again a local person who is supposed to know better) who was taking his catch to the public market. The onset of symptoms took little more than an hour. This time each member of the crew of six immediately took a charcoal poisoning-prevention packet like those given to kids who consume dangerous household cleansers, etc. It might be that the charcoal worked to absorb the toxin or maybe the fish we ate was less toxic, but the symptoms were less severe and our recovery was faster than the first encounter with ciguatera poisoning. However our new Aussie crew member, who had consumed the most fish (his first poisoning), became very ill. After several days on the boat, he eventually required a stay in the village infirmary and a month's recuperation.

For cruisers sailing in tropical areas, here are some suggestions related to ciguatera poisoning:

◆Use caution when eating fish caught in tropical waters.
◆Avoid eating fish considered harmful by local people.

- ◆Avoid eating large predatory fish like groupers, barracuda, snappers, and jacks. The larger the fish, the more toxin it is likely to have absorbed.
- ◆The head and viscera and roe are places with increased toxicity.
- ◆Do not eat local fish after any damage or disturbance to the reef areas.
- ◆It is best to eat fish caught on the leeward side of islands.
- ◆No known antitoxin exists, but Mannitol (intravenous medication) has proven effective as a treatment.
- ◆You can become infected by eating fish in restaurants.
- ◆Ciguatoxin is not affected (killed) by heat or freezing.
- ◆Fish caught well offshore are more likely to be free of ciguatera poisoning.

HawaiiChemtect of Pasadena, CA (818-568-8606) is developing a test to determine whether a fish is contaminated with ciguatoxin. The test materials (test strips and chemicals) require refrigeration and are best suited to land use. Their research, though, yields a possible onboard test that could be valuable to the mariner.

While cleaning the fish, retain the liver. Rub the raw liver on your lips or tongue (it's really not so bad!) and if they begin to tingle after a few moments, discard the fish. Avoid the fish entrails and roe which will always contain the highest amount of toxin.

Another solution is to have one crew member eat a very small piece of the fish and see what happens! You'll have to wait an hour or two (sometimes longer). We tried this several times while cruising in the Caribbean. Anna and I alternated being the ship's taster—but never detected any problems.

Mannitol is the only known treatment for ciguatera poisoning. It is both effective and safe, but it must be administered intravenously and therefore requires an experienced medical practitioner. The average cruiser would not be trained for this eventuality, but you could learn. The dosage (as noted in the *JAMA* May 13, 1988—Vol 259, NO. 18 report) was no more than 250ml of 20% mannitol given intravenously; the rate of infusion was 1 g/kg given over 30 minutes in a piggyback manner.

Even if you are not qualified to administer this treatment, you might still be smart to try to carry some on board; if your crew should ever be stricken, try to find someone to administer it. In this and similar situations, you might also get medical expertise by radio if an emergency finds you in remote locations.

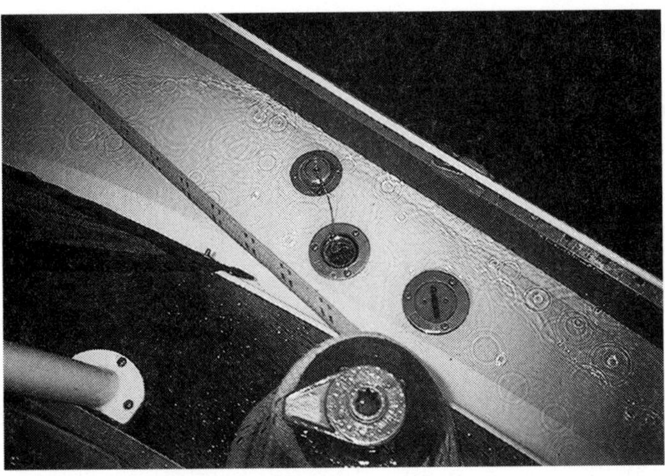

The easy way to fill your water tanks: just open your deck fill during a squall or rain storm.

Water-Catchment Methods

Develop a water-catchment system for your boat. In squalls or during the rainy season, a good rain can often fill the tanks. Some boats use special awnings for this purpose. Underway, some boats catch water off the sails when it runs to the gooseneck. Others only have to open the fresh-water fill cap in their deck and let the water run in. Let it rain for a few minutes to clean the sails and deck of salt water and then try your hand—it's one of the few free things left. Sometimes you can go for weeks without worrying about jugging or making water. Don't forget to add your chlorine bleach.

Roaches, Rats, and Mildew

These pests in paradise are not a big problem, but boats sailing in the tropics are occasionally subject to infestations of roaches and/or rats. Although some roaches fly, others board your boat while it's tied to a dock or pier. Some come onboard via your moorings lines. This is true also of rats. But most roaches are brought aboard by you—while provisioning the boat. They live and reproduce in the containers and cardboard boxes you use to carry aboard ship's stores. Even if there are no live roaches, there may be roach eggs that will hatch in the future aboard your boat. A good rule is to never bring packaging materials on the boat, and thoroughly wash everything ashore first—using salt water if necessary. Large stalks of bananas should be dragged in the sea before being placed aboard.

If you find you have roaches, one way to deal with them is by mixing sweetened cream with boric acid (in powdered form from the pharmacy). Fill small plastic bottle caps with the thick paste and distribute these around the boat where you think the roaches are hiding. If you don't have bottle caps, mix the paste thick, like dough, and roll it into small pill-sized balls which can then be placed about the boat. This should take care of the situation. Don't let the roaches multiply. Get on the problem fast and you won't have a big problem.

You can keep you boat free of the pests most of the time. Borax mixed with a little sugar and sprinkled around the galley is also effective for roaches. Keep a spray can of roach killer handy to get the ones you might meet in person.

Most boats never get rats, but carry a big rat trap just in case. If one should get below decks, you can't use poison because it may die in some inaccessible place on your boat—that's the reason for the extra large rat trap—just don't step on it on the salon floor some dark night!

You can have mildew problems if your boat stays in warm, humid conditions long enough. The best preventative is lot of fresh air and periodic wipe-downs with vinegar or ammonia.

Chapter 8

Reference Section

Anchors and Ground Tackle

Whole books are written about ground tackle. Every skipper has his or her favorite choice of anchors and strong opinions about anchoring techniques. My list of equipment is an all-purpose listing that should find you prepared for most cruising situations, but not for the ultimate storm nor for extended high-latitude cruising. It should give you a starting point and general parameters for this most important equipment category.

Most of the time you will be anchoring on one hook. Once away from crowded anchorages, you will find yourself generally swinging on a single anchor. It's often a chore to set and retrieve two hooks set bow and stern, and it generally does nothing to improve the safety of your boat in normal anchoring situations. It slows your reaction time to sudden weather changes and does not allow your boat to swing with wind and tide. This, in turn, places extra strain on all your ground tackle and encourages rode chafe on rollers and cleats.

The only times to use anchors bow and stern are in an anchorage too small to allow the boat to swing with the tide, or in a spot where other boats are already riding on bow and stern hooks. In this case you must select your spot carefully and do the same. If you want to use only one anchor, you must position yourself far enough away from other boats to avoid swinging into them—as you will probably do when the wind or tide changes. Anchoring protocol requires that you follow the lead of the first boat anchored—or stay clear.

Two hooks can hold your boat in the middle of a tight anchorage, but the prudent skipper should always be prepared to buoy the stern anchor and throw it clear for later retrieval. Be ready to leave it if the weather turns against you. Your ground tackle can be retrieved later. Be sure your marking buoy carries your boat name and ID.

For most mid-latitude cruising, you will need two anchors available at the bow and one at the stern. The second anchor deployed from the bow is for increased security in a blow or to reduce swinging room and yawing. In addition you'll need a larger storm anchor in reserve. Use your storm anchor for bad weather or in case one of your working anchors is lost. Also, carry one of those little folding grapnel-type anchors for the dinghy. You will use this more than you think.

As mentioned earlier, on your working anchor/s at the bow, you should have at least one pound of anchor for each foot of boat, and one foot of chain for each foot of boat. At the stern, where you may have to retrieve it by dinghy, you can use a smaller and lighter hook such as a *Danforth*-type.

General Ground Tackle Rules

For Principal Working Anchor (typical 40' cruising boat, sail or power)

- ◆ One pound of anchor/foot of boat. (40' boat = 40- to 45-pound anchor)
- ◆ One foot of chain/foot of boat. (40' boat needs at least 40' 3/8" BBB chain, if you're not using all chain.
- ◆ Use 200' to 300' of 3-strand nylon. (40' boat needs at least 5/8" rode)
- ◆ Use a swivel to avoid hockles. Place it between nylon rode and chain (or between chain and anchor on all-chain systems.
- ◆ Wire all shackles and swivels closed. Use Monel or stainless steel wire.
- ◆ Secure the bitter end to the boat, or you could lose the whole system.
- ◆ Mark the rode. Use black plastic electrical wire ties to mark each 25 feet of rode or chain. Insert the wire tie through the rope or chain. Repeat for each additional 100 feet of rode or chain, but on successive 100-foot sections, alternate between black and white wire ties, for even easier depth reading.

1 tie = 25 feet	3 ties = 75 feet
2 ties = 50 feet	4 ties = 100 feet

For Stern, Storm, or Second Bow Anchors

- Scale the size and type of anchor, rode, and chain up or down for different uses and for differing bottom conditions.

Bitter End

There are lots of jokes about the bitter end of an anchor rode, and probably many of them are true. The onboard end of your rode should always be secured below decks, somewhere in the chain locker, to avoid losing the bitter end overboard in an anchoring snafu, hence your whole rig would be a total loss. An anchor system secured in this fashion is fine if you use nylon rode. But if you use all chain, like most cruisers do, it could lead to problems if you need to quickly leave an anchorage, for example, to avoid a fast developing and dangerous weather situation. It can't be done quickly if your anchor rode is all chain and the bitter end is secured below.

The answer is to attach a short line to the end of the chain that normally stays aboard, just long enough to allow the bitter end of the chain to come on deck but remain secured by the line from below. Now, with a knife you could quickly cut the line to free yourself from the chain and ground tackle in an emergency. If you have time, try to buoy the bitter end before it goes overboard, so that you can retrieve your ground tackle later.

Anchor Types

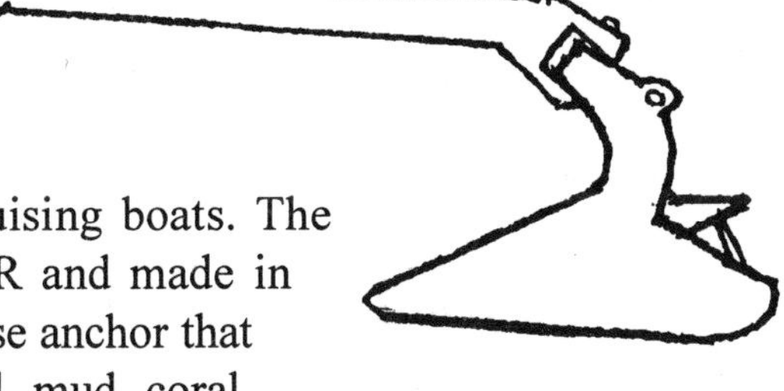

Plow Anchors

Plow anchors are the most commonly found anchors on cruising boats. The original is manufactured by CQR and made in Scotland. It is a rugged, all-purpose anchor that holds well in most bottoms (sand, mud, coral, and rock) and stows easily on your bow. The only times I have had a problem setting a plow anchor is on a hard bottom covered with insufficient sand or on a bottom covered with eel grass where the anchor just wouldn't dig in and set. (Please note: This type of bottom is frequently found in the Red Sea and the Mediterranean.) A plow is rugged, not easily bent, resets as the boat swings on a single hook, and will bury itself deeper and deeper if stressed. *Delta* is a new model CQR with no moving parts that is designed for self launching and stowing when coupled with a remotely operated windlass.

Danforth Anchors

Danforths are the backup anchors of choice for many boats. In soft mud and sand they will hold better than a plow. Because of their design and large fluke area, they can be lighter than the plow yet still provide the same holding power. Smaller Danforths can be easily rowed out in a dinghy for a second bower, or set from the stern when bow and stern anchoring is required to limit swinging. Because of their light weight, they can be more easily retrieved from your dinghy. Danforths don't stow on the bow as neatly as do plow-type anchors. But for small cruising boats, their light weight could make them the anchor of first choice. Because of their lighter construction, their flukes can be bent if caught in rocks or coral—so don't buy cheap substitutes. Danforths will bury, reset on tidal changes, and hold when sometimes other anchors won't. On my own 37-foot sloop, whenever I had trouble setting the 45-pound plow, my 22-pound Danforth usually did the job. For a stern hook I used a 12-pound high test model. Original Danforths come in standard and hi-test models. The Fortress is an aluminum Danforth-type anchor made in Florida. It has tested near the top for holding power in recent anchor tests and is very light weight. A large storm anchor of this type could be disassembled and kept in the bilge until needed.

Bruce Anchors

Bruce anchors are in many ways similar to the plows—strong and easily set. This anchor is one piece (no moving parts), very strong, and on many boats is used as the principal anchor. Bruce advocates claim they can hang on shorter scope and retrieve their hooks more easily than other anchors. Like the plow, they are good in most bottoms, except eel grass and hard shale. Bruce anchors, because of their unique design, sometimes pose stowage problems on the foredeck or when secured on the bow rollers for passagemaking.

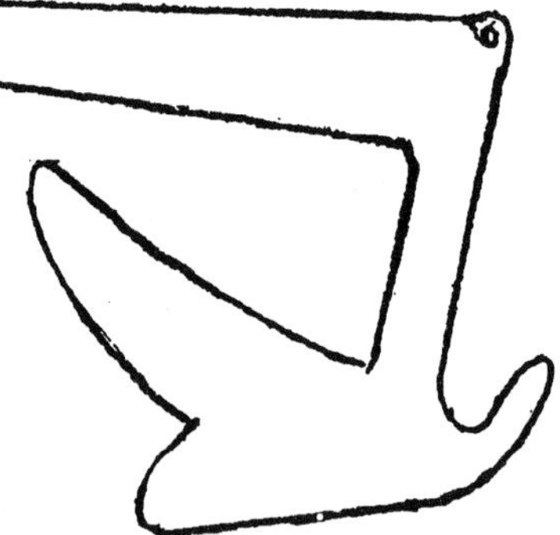

Practical Sailor magazine recently tested anchors and found the Bruce's reliability to be questionable in strong winds because of its tendency to break out and then reset again. If this occurred while you were asleep, it could cause a boat to walk downwind without the skipper's knowing about it.

Fisherman or Yachtsman Anchors

For some bottoms, the traditional fisherman's or yachtsman's anchor will hold where nothing else seems to set properly. In heavy eel grass or on hard shale when other anchors sometime have a hard time setting, the fisherman or a Danforth may work well. In the Mediterranean, cruisers use the fisherman anchor extensively. Its downside is that it is heavy and hard to stow. Two other anchors that are recommended by Med cruisers are the Max and the German Bo anchor. I've not used either of them, but you might check them out if you're planning to cruise the Mediterranean.

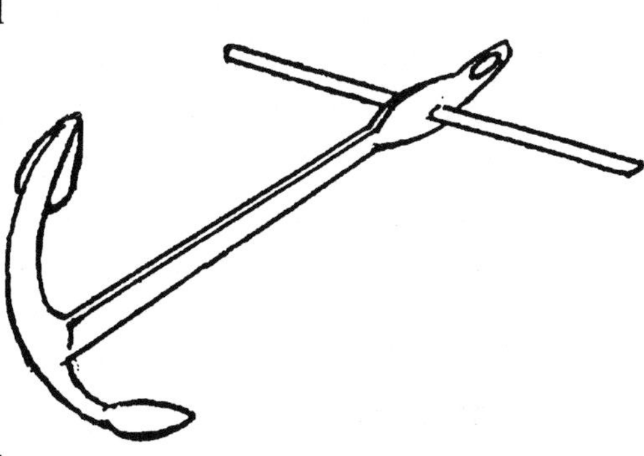

Anchoring Techniques

Explore the Anchorage

Don't be in a big hurry to get your hook down. Slowly power around the anchorage while checking depth, swinging room, and watching for underwater hazards. Look carefully at all previously anchored boats to determine which way their anchor rodes lead out. This step can tell you much about the tide, current, or wind now affecting boats in the anchorage. Notice if the other boats are riding on one or two hooks. How are their anchors deployed? Bow and stern, two off the bow, or hopefully just one off the bow. If you choose to anchor here, you will have to do the same. How much scope do they have out? If you anchor nearby, you will have to use a similar amount. Will there be room for you without squeezing in and creating problems? Previously anchored boats are notoriously territorial. Try to avoid anything that could appear to be confrontational. The first boat at anchor sets the rules for boats that follow.

Picking the Spot to Drop your Anchor

After thoroughly checking the anchorage area, you will by now have selected the best spot to drop the anchor. It should give you protection from expected winds and seas, allow you to swing through 360° with tidal changes, and keep you well clear of other boats and obstructions. Once your drop-point is determined, mentally move your boat back to the spot where it will lie after you have set the anchor and let out your full scope. Is this where you will be clear of dangers, avoid problems with other boats, and where you will feel comfortable? If so, it is now time to start the actual anchoring process.

Swinging Characteristics

The swinging characteristics of other boats already at anchor are frequently overlooked when you're choosing a spot to drop the hook. While you are slowly reconnoitering through the anchorage, picking the best available spot, you must be aware of the very different swinging manners of various kinds of boats. Powerboats and multihulls will respond much more to wind than will a deep-keeled sailboat. Monohull sailboats will respond more to current and tidal changes. Boats on all chain will swing less to wind and current and lie closer to their anchors than those on nylon rodes. A boat on two anchors will move about very little and must be avoided unless you plan to do the same. All these factors must be considered when picking a spot—if you want to avoid those late night "anchor conferences" when the tide changes or the wind picks up.

Scope

The books all say 7:1 scope is the best for holding, meaning the rode length should be seven times the water depth. And they are right. The problem is that you will very rarely get that kind of swinging room in an anchorage—especially with other boats around. You will probably have to settle for 5:1, 4:1 or even 3:1 scope. This is generally perfectly adequate for most situations with good bottom-holding characteristics. As your anchoring skills are refined, you will develop a feel for the right scope in different anchoring situations. You will know when to put out more scope or when to set a second anchor. If you use all chain, you may be able to use less scope for any given situation, because the weight and catenary of chain keeps it closer to the bottom than does nylon rode.

Anchoring in Reverse

If you are planning to anchor from the bow and then back down to set your anchor, which is the most commonly used method, proceed forward very slowly to your selected anchoring spot. Stop the boat completely and begin backing down in the same direction as nearby boats lying to their anchors. As your boat just begins to move in reverse, drop your anchor to the bottom and slowly let the boat pull the chain from the locker and lay it on the bottom. You want the rode and/or chain to lie in a long line on the bottom and not be piled on top of the anchor—where it could tangle and cause problems. Keep your speed under one knot while anchoring. Do this deliberately—too much boat speed is your enemy here.

Setting the Anchor

While still laying out your rode or chain, gradually and carefully put a light strain on the rode to start the process of setting and digging in your anchor. Do this a little at a time until you are nearly at your planned maximum scope, based on the water depth. Too much speed now will just pull the anchor along the bottom and not allow it to set. Very slowly, with the boat in neutral or slow reverse, "fish" the hook into the bottom to continue the setting process. Slowly bring up the engine power to gradually set the anchor into the seabed.

As the engine power is carefully increased, you should start taking visual bearings abeam to determine if the boat is dragging. If the boat seems to be holding, gradually increase the power to approximate the pressure of a strong wind—about the RPM of the boat while traveling at full cruising speed. It is much better to determine now if the anchor is holding, rather than in the middle of the night. If you start to drag, reduce power immediately and allow the anchor to settle in for a few more minutes. Then let out a little more scope and try the setting process again—even more slowly. Many times a second or third attempt will do the trick. If you still drag, you will have to pick up the anchor and start the whole process over—perhaps in a new spot. Eventually you will get a feel for setting the anchor, but it may take some work on your part. "Practice makes perfect" certainly is true when anchoring. Before departure on your cruise, take an afternoon and go practice anchoring. It will pay dividends, and in the process you will develop teamwork and coordination between the anchor person and the helmsperson.

The Anchor Snubber

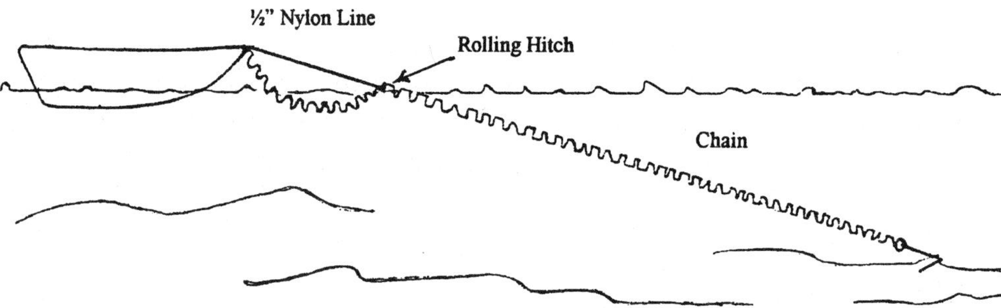

If you use all chain on your anchor (highly recommended), the final thing you need to do, after setting the anchor and taking bearings, is to attach a nylon snubber on the chain. This will transfer the load from the windlass to a mooring cleat, reduce any noise that could come aboard via the chain, and impart elasticity to an all-chain anchoring system.

To do this, all you need is a piece of nylon line about 35 feet long connected to the chain on one end and the other end made fast to a cleat on the bow. The line shouldn't be heavier than about ½ inch, because you want maximum stretch. Special chain hooks are available to streamline the connection to the chain, but I much prefer to simply tie a rolling hitch directly on the chain. This hitch will not chafe, slip off, or chip the galvanizing like a chain hook sometimes will. Secure the other end of the snubber to the ship's mooring cleat. Now let out a bit more chain so that the strain is taken on the snubber, with the chain hanging in a loose loop below. This will allow the snubber to stretch and provide the desired dampening effect. Attaching the snubber should take no more then a minute or two.

Anchoring While Moving Forward

You don't see this done often, but if your boat is reluctant to steer in reverse, as mine is, try this technique. While moving forward very slowly, drop your bow anchor in the previously selected spot and proceed in the direction you expect the boat to lie. When you have deployed sufficient scope (four to five times the water depth), start to set the anchor by increasing tension with the windlass clutch or by hand. Be careful and go slowly, because you will have the weight of the whole boat to slow or stop. As the anchor digs in, it will gradually bring to a stop the slowly moving boat and swing it around 180° pointing back toward the spot you originally dropped the anchor. You have now set the anchor, stretched out the rode/chain, and are probably lying about where you expected. Adjust your rode to the desired scope and cleat it down.

Tie on the snubber and you're finished. You can also use this or similar techniques to set an anchor under sail.

If you try the forward-setting technique, here is a word of caution. In very shoal anchorages under 15 feet, powering forward while anchoring from the bow will bring the rode or anchor chain near the propeller underwater. I have never had a problem with this, but skippers should use caution to avoid wrapping the prop.

Taking Bearings

While setting your anchor, take visual bearings abeam to see if you are dragging. This will determine whether you are holding or not. When it looks and feels like your anchor is firmly set, gradually increase the engine RPMs to really stress it. It is much better for the boat to drag or break loose now, rather than later—when you're off in the dinghy or sound asleep. If the wind starts to blow later, take another set of bearings.

Use your hand bearing compass or sight over the binnacle. Compare them later with additional similar bearings to see if you're still holding. If your boat has radar, you may be able to use its alarm feature to tell if you're dragging. The alarm feature on your GPS may work in this situation too.

Yawing

If your anchored boat starts yawing in a blow, meaning it sails back and forth on its anchor, try dropping your second bow anchor at the top (extreme end) of one of those swings. This second hook should not line up with the first anchor, but should be as far as possible to either side. When you set it, it will have much less scope than the primary anchor. But even so, it can greatly reduce the amount of yawing, lessen the strain on your ground tackle, and possibly keep your anchor from breaking out. When departing the next day, pick up this second and probably smaller anchor first, then retrieve the main anchor.

Anchor Retrieval

When it's time to pick up the anchor or anchors, slowly power toward the original drop spot while the bowman retrieves the rode or chain. Make the boat do the work here, not the windlass motor or your back. Use hand signals. The helmsperson will not be able to follow the rode, which may snake around the bottom, from his/her cockpit location—so give hand directions. Pick up and retrieve the rode only when it's hanging nearly straight down from the bow. When the boat is almost over the anchor, cleat down the rode or chain

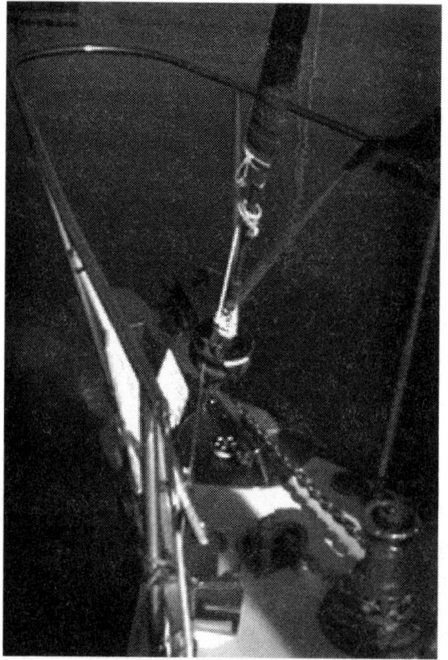

After retrieving the anchor, you'll be glad you installed a wash-down pump.

and allow the weight and motion of the boat to slowly break out the anchor. After the anchor is freed, it can easily be hauled to the bow and stowed. If you've anchored in mud, you will bless your decision to install a wash-down pump to hose off the chain and anchor as it's hauled aboard.

If you have set two anchors equidistant from the bow and one is all chain, it is best to pick up this one first. It is easier if you get the chain off the bottom before trying to maneuver the boat over the second anchor.

Quiet Anchoring—Using Hand Signals

I've not seen many boats use hand signals when anchoring, but visual signals work great and avoid lots of shouting between the cockpit and the foredeck. You can actually anchor your boat without saying a word! Below are the signals we use on our boat. Add to them if you want, or make up your own.

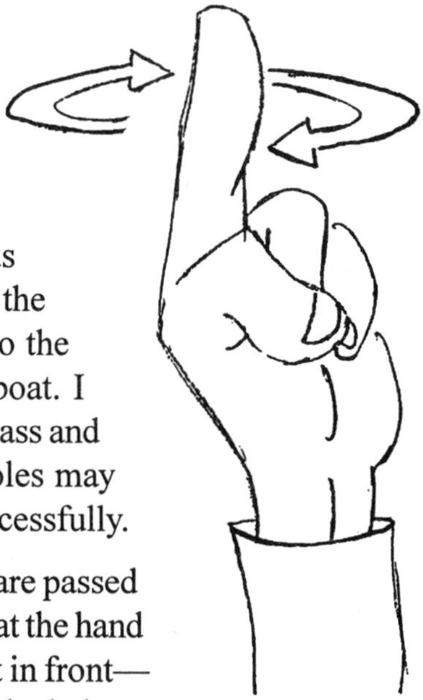

If you want to try them, the first thing to do is work out the sight lines aboard your own boat—to be sure there is continuous visual communication between the person on the bow and the helmsperson. On our boat, I do the anchoring and my wife, Anna, drives the boat. I prefer handling the chain, anchors, and windlass and Anna prefers to steer. On other boats the roles may be reversed. I've seen it work both ways successfully.

Anchoring signals originate on the bow and are passed to the helmsperson as necessary. Take care that the hand signals are made at the side of the body—not in front—so they can easily be seen by the person on the helm.

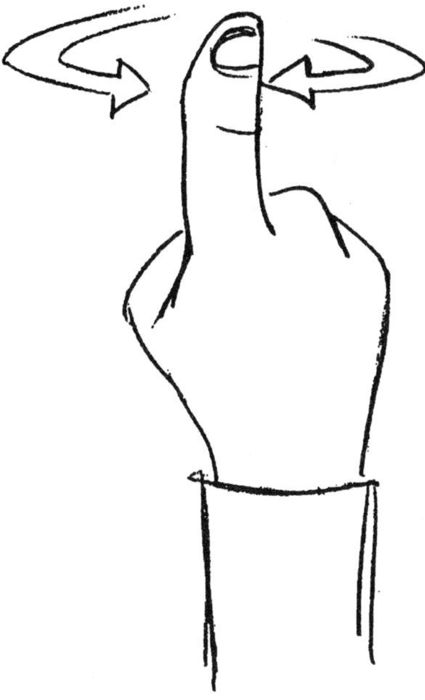

Forward Power...Speed determined by the speed of the hand signal.

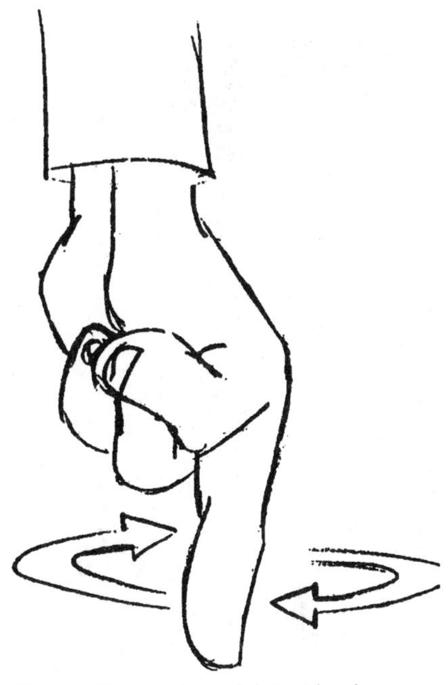

Reverse Power...Speed determined by the speed of the hand signal.

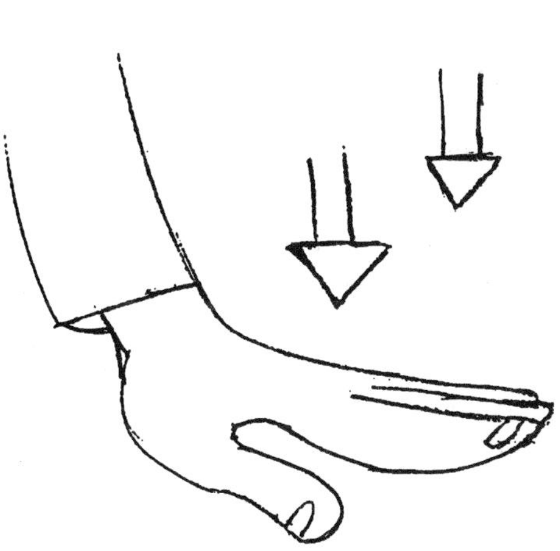

Slow Down & Reduce Speed

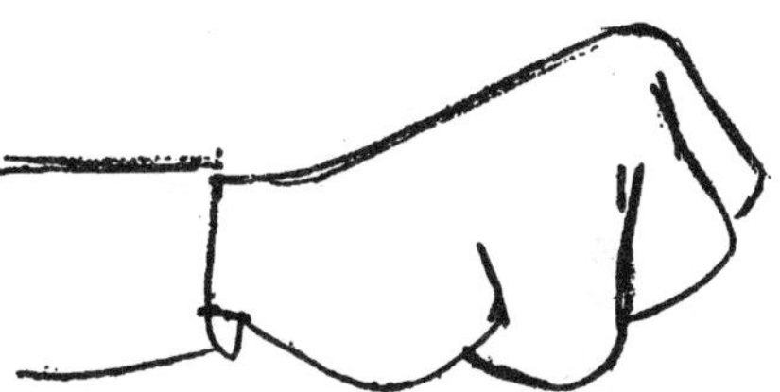

Hold This Position...Use engine controls to keep boat in this spot.

Cut The Engine...(Signal as if cutting throat.)

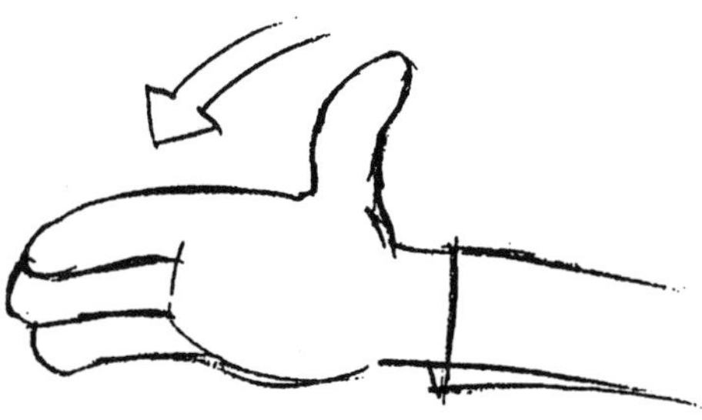

Steer Left...follow my hand direction.

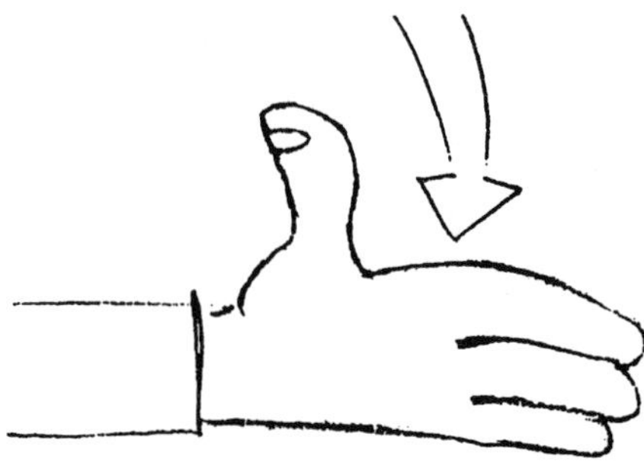

Steer Right...follow my hand direction.

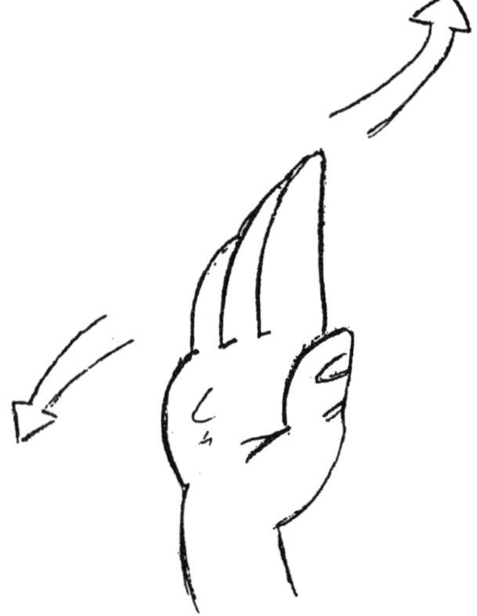

Stright Ahead...follow my hand direction.

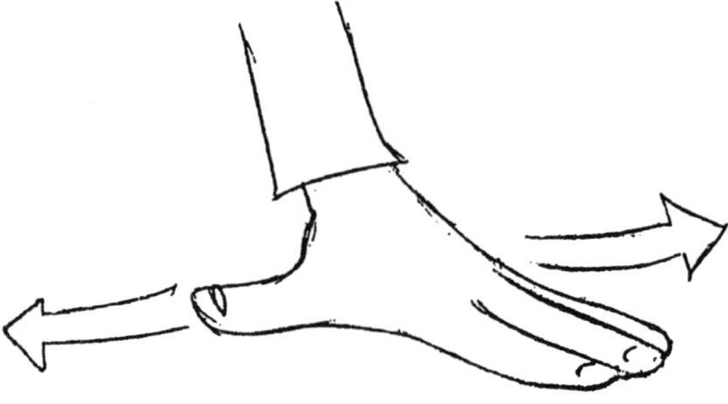

Anchor Is Off Bottom...boat can now be slowly maneuvered as necessary.

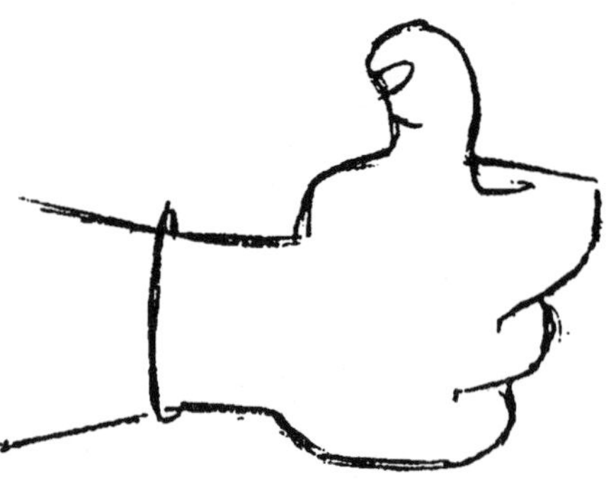

Anchor Is Secure...proceed as necessary, free to increase speed.

QUIET ANCHORING SIGNALS
from the person handling the anchor to the person on the helm.

Dinghy Accessories—Security and Landing Techniques

Security

In many of the places you might cruise, a new dinghy and motor are coveted items that are prized by native fisherman and others who live near the sea. These are items that many in the community could never hope to own. Where thievery is a problem, the marine radio nets will most likely alert you as you approach those areas. The loss of a dinghy and outboard motor creates a major problem for the cruiser due to loss of mobility and the difficulty of finding suitable replacements in remote areas—not to mention the substantial costs involved. Compounding the problem is the fact that most cruising boats just don't have room to carry a spare dinghy and motor.

If you go south to Central and South America (and probably lots of other areas too), in some places you will need to lock you dinghy when you take it ashore and hoist it out of the water on a halyard when you turn in at night.

Mooring and Security Cables

Plan to rig a coated SS cable (Use Nico Press sleeve fittings and their small portable pressing tool.) from your towing eyes at the front of the dinghy long enough (25 to 30 feet) to be used as an alternate painter (mooring line) from the bow. A cable size of 1/8-inch or 3/16-inch is about right. If you have any doubts about security, padlock the dinghy wherever you leave it. Run a smaller second cable through the gas tank and outboard motor, and lock it to a through-bolted padeye on the dinghy's transom. Drill holes through your oars so you can lock them up too. Lead the free end of this cable loosely forward to permanently connect with the security cable at the bow. Now, anyone wanting to take your dinghy or motor will have to carry cable cutters—uncommon in many areas.

Dinghy lifted on bridle for security.

Lifting Bridles

At night, most cruisers find a way to hoist their dinghies (motor attached) four to six feet out of the water. Any attempt to steal it from this position is likely to dissuade potential thieves and encourage them to look for easier targets—like dinghies tied with line and streamed aft of the boat during the night. You will need to make a 3- or 4-point bridle with coated SS wire. This will attach to the bow at the towing eye (or other strong points) and to two pad eyes in the transom. Adjust the bridle so that the dinghy hangs a bit down-by-the-stern, so that in a heavy rain the water will drain out and not tear the dinghy loose. Be sure you remove the drain plug each night—and replace it again the next morning before launching. Forgetting the first could require a midnight trip on deck in a thunderstorm, and forgetting the second will necessitate bailing the dinghy and flushing out the motor if it should break loose because of the extra weight.

Dinghy Wheels

It may seem strange to talk about installing wheels on your dinghy. But for the cruiser, dinghy wheels solve problems for which there are no other solutions. After you dinghy to shore, how do you move a 10-foot inflatable or hard dinghy with an 8- to10-HP motor above the high-tide line? It's just too heavy and can't easily be done by mom and pop cruisers unless it is equipped with wheels. How do you land and re-launch successfully on a beach with breaking waves without getting dumped in the surf? You can learn how if you have wheels. See Chapter 4, ***Outfitting Your Vessel for Cruising—Dinghies*** for more on dinghy wheels.

Towing Bridles

In addition to the large inflatable dinghy wheels, you will probably need to install a 3-point towing bridle. This is standard on some inflatable dinghies and an extra on others. If you need to add them, you can buy the manufacturer's optional towing patches separately and then adhere them on the boat yourself. Since you will probably be towing the dink a lot, you need the extra strength of a towing bridal to prevent it from ripping loose from the dinghy when underway. When you're going six knots, try pulling in the towed dinghy. You'll find that there is a lot of tension on the line and lots of strain on the towing eyes of the dinghy.

Sun protection can double the life of your dinghy.

Covers

In the tropics, protect everything you can from the sun. This is especially true of inflatable dinghies—the sun just eats them up. It really helps to apply 303 or Armor All. Get an easy-to-install cover made that protects the top and sides of your dinghy. Have bungee-cord sewn around the bottom so it will snap easily over the boat. A few grommets around the bottom will allow for cross ties when necessary. Use it for sun protection and also to keep out rain water. If you lash the dinghy on the foredeck for short passages, stow it upside down to avoid having it filled in a seaway. Even when it's upside down, protect you dinghy with the cover—it should fit the dinghy this way too. A cover will greatly extend your dinghy's life and pay for itself several times over.

Ditch Bag

In remote places, it's a mistake to go exploring in the dinghy without considering the "what if" possibilities. Be sure to take the oars, dinghy anchor, life vests, and extra gas. Before venturing far away from the main boat, prepare a mini-dinghy-ditch-bag. It should contain a waterproof flashlight, whistle, hand-held VHF, a bottle of water, and maybe a knife and a couple of hand-held flares. Inside your engine cowling, secure the tool kit that came with the outboard motor—there's generally plenty of room. It should contain a screw driver, pliers, spare spark plugs, spark plug wrench, and an extra starting cord.

Landing Technique with Wheels

Use the following techniques to land and launch through moderate surf (usually successfully. Our dinghy was an Avon 310 powered with an 8-HP Tohatsu. This dinghy performed well and held up for five years in the tropics—in fact, we still use it. The outboard motor, also still in use, is tough and provides ample power to plane the boat with two people and snorkel gear. The dinghy is equipped with large 16-inch pneumatic wheels that allow it to be driven ashore without worrying about the propeller. See Chapter 10, ***Contacts*** for suppliers of dinghy wheels.)

Wheels on dinghy can make beach landings a one-person job.

When going ashore, stop just outside the surf line and lower your wheels into position. With wheels in the water your boat speed will be slower—but still much faster than you could row. Wait as long as necessary to note the sets of waves and get a feel for their timing. What you're looking for is the slack period between the sets. Look both ashore and out to sea. You can see the waves beginning to form, pass under the dinghy, and finally where they begin to curl and break. When, while looking out to sea, you cannot see new waves forming (the slack between the sets), throttle up and start for the beach. If you're following a wave in—that okay; just don't overtake it. Ride the wave as far up the beach as you can. The person in the bow should be prepared to hop out with the painter in hand and keep a strain on the bow so it doesn't wash out with the retreating wave. Since the stern will now be resting on the wheels with the prop mostly out of the water, the helmsman can cut the engine and hop out too. Lift the bow and pull the dinghy up the beach to a secure position, and lock it around a palm tree. You made it! Note that it was never necessary to raise the motor—leave it in the down position if you like.

Launching Techniques with Wheels

When it comes time to head back to your boat, the procedure is a little different. It again requires watching and timing the surf. Don't get impatient. Just wait until the time is right. With wheels and engine down, back your dinghy into shallow water (stern first) and have the helmsman hop in and prepare to start the motor. Sometimes you can actually start it now while waiting, but remember that the motor needs its cooling water. The person at the bow, who is standing in shallow water and facing the waves, holds the stern squarely to the incoming waves and pushes slowly out as far as possible without getting all wet. When the last wave breaks from the present set and you can see the slack water out to sea, the bow person pushes hard and jumps in. While this is going on, the motor is started, and the boat is quickly backed into deep water, where it's finally turned to face any new waves or swells forming in the next set. Out beyond the surf line, you can bring up the wheels if you need more speed for the return trip to your anchored boat. If not, just leave them down. The whole process—from the time the bowman pushes off to the time you turn the dinghy to face the waves—should take no more than 10 to 20 seconds.

The above dinghy procedures can be used even without wheels on your transom. But you will have to take care to raise the motor in time so as not to the damage the propeller when landing. Once ashore, you and your mate will have to carry the dinghy and engine up the beach—a heavy chore. On re-launch, the person on the bow will have a harder time holding the stern into the waves and probably get wet in the process.

U.S. and Foreign Nautical Charts

NOAA

National Oceanographic and Atmospheric Administration: Publishes charts of U.S. coastal waters.

DMA

Defense Mapping Administration: Publishes U.S. charts of international waters.

Imray Charts

Private British publishing company: Publishes Caribbean charts edited by Donald Street. These are excellent charts for small boat navigation, considered the best available in the Caribbean.

British Admiralty Charts

Publishes high quality world-wide British charts. Addresses some areas not covered by U.S. charts. More expensive than domestic charts.

French Charts

Best charts for French portions of the South Pacific and French home waters. Expensive.

Electronic Charts

Electronic charts are here. You can get the whole U.S. Atlantic or Pacific coast on a single CD ROM. If you choose to go this way, you must back up your navigation system with reliable paper charts and knowledgeable plotting practices. Electronics don't like the marine environment very well, and you could be in serious trouble if any of the vulnerable parts should fail. Most of the serious cruisers have electronic failures at some point during their time afloat, and you just can't afford to take the risk with the safety of your boat and crew.

Pilot Charts

Published by U.S. for all oceans in several editions. Pilot charts are not charts in the usual sense and are not designed for plotting your course. They are used for gathering information relating to a specific body of water. The frequency of storms, prevailing wind direction and strength, the average wave heights, and even the water temperature are just a few of the matters graphically depicted. In tropical waters, the frequency and typical tracks of tropical storms and hurricanes are plotted.

Pilot charts are published for specific months—sometimes monthly, sometimes quarterly, and sometimes packaged in yearly catalogs. They are published for all oceans and are more or less permanent charts, because the material depicted represents information gathered over many years. They do not need yearly updates to retain their value to the cruising sailor. Be sure you have this invaluable resource onboard.

Chart Catalogs

Chart catalogs are published by NOAA (NOS) and DMA. They describe and list available U.S. charts for both U.S. and international waters. These listings are very helpful in planning itineraries and determining necessary chart purchases. By perusing and studying chart catalogs you can determine what charts you need for the cruise you are planning. Chart catalogs are available free from most chart suppliers. Since chart catalogues are organized regionally and geographically, some cruisers use them as a tool to organize and maintain their own onboard charts rather than develop their own computer listing.

Chart Scale

You've probably heard the terms "large scale" and "small scale" applied to charts. These terms are important since they describe the amount of detail and the size of the area depicted on various charts. If you remember a slightly longer version of this description, it will be more helpful in your selection of charts for your own voyaging. Remember this instead: ***Large Scale-Small Area*** charts give a great deal of detail for a small area. A harbor chart would be a good example; it gives a lot of detailed information about a small area—perfect for entering a new harbor. The actual scale might be 1:10,000 (large scale), meaning a single unit of measurement on the chart is equal to 10,000 of those units on the surface of the globe. A ***Small Scale-Large Area*** chart is just the opposite. It shows very little detail, but it covers a large oceanic area. The scale might be 1:1,500,000 (small scale), showing a large oceanic area. This kind of chart would be great to plan routes for an upcoming passage—but useless for entering a strange anchorage. Study your chart catalogs carefully for the charts you will need. Each chart description will include the chart name, the scale, and the latest edition available.

Allow a good deal of time to peruse chart catalogs: NOAA for U.S. coastal waters, and DMA for international waters. These catalogs give cruisers an amazing amount of information about available charts, about chart scales (the area and scale depicted on the chart), and about other nautical matters of interest to cruisers. They are government publications and available free of charge at most stores supplying nautical charts.

For international waters, frequently you'll find alternatives to U.S. charts. They are even more expensive than the U.S. versions but are sometimes considered superior to DMA charts of the same waters, so they should be considered. Check with other cruisers who have already sailed these waters for their recommendations. Such is the case in the Caribbean where Imray charts are preferred for small-craft cruising. In Polynesia, French charts are generally considered superior to their U.S. versions.

Photocopying Charts

Since U.S. charts are not copyrighted, copies can be made on large photocopiers at less than half the original cost. These copies are much better than nothing, but if copied in black and white they lose the significance of color from their original editions. Such charts are considerably harder to read. They also will not be printed on the same heavy-duty chart paper that defies the elements and withstands erasures and abuse. In areas depicting only natural features and coastline, you may prefer used charts. They are sold between cruisers for about $4 to $6 dollars each. Just remember that the navigational aids and lights on out-of-date charts will almost certainly be wrong, but land masses, coastlines and natural features will probably not have changed much. The latest chart date is found in the lower left corner of U.S. charts. In more civilized areas where there are man-made structures and navigational aids, the cruiser is well advised to acquire recent charts and cruising guides.

Preserving Food without Refrigeration -- by Anna Gleckler

If you're a do-it-yourselfer or if you're planning a long cruise, particularly to remote areas, you may want to try your hand at food preservation techniques that require no refrigeration—long used by voyaging sailors.

Waxing Cheese

Waxing works best on hard cheeses such as parmesan, provolone, Romano and aged gouda. Slightly softer cheeses like cheddar and jack can also be kept waxed. Wipe each block lightly with vinegar and wrap in one layer of cheese cloth which also has been dipped in vinegar. Melt three pounds of paraffin for each 10 pounds of cheese. Use a double boiler; an old coffee can works great and is disposable. Dip one half of each block into the melted paraffin and allow it to dry completely before dipping the other half. Each block should be coated with five coats of wax. It will last for many months.

Brining Butter or Margarine

Press butter or margarine into a sterilized wide-mouth glass jar to within one inch of the top. Squeeze out all air bubbles. Completely fill each jar with a brine solution made by mixing ¼ cup of salt with 2 cup of water. Cap each jar with a sterilized seal and lid. Lasts up to six months.

Making Jerky

Use lean meat and trim away all fat, because fat can turn rancid and ruin the meat. A beef flank steak is a good cut for making jerky. Cut meat with the grain into ¼-inch strips. Cover strips with soy sauce or your own marinade and soak overnight.

Solar Drying: Drain the meat and place on plates. The air temperature should be above 50° F. Leave it in direct sunlight for three days, turning it occasionally. Bring the meat inside at night and during rainy periods. After three days outside, place the meat in an oven and further dry for one hour at 175° F. When properly cured and cooled, it will appear shriveled and black, and it will crack when broken. There should be no beads of moisture on the broken edges. If stowed in glass containers, jerky should last a year.

Overnight Drying: Place drained meat strips ½ inch apart directly on oven racks or cookie sheets. Slowly cook the beef in a 120° F oven for five hours. Turn the strips and cook for another four hours. Cool and store in jars.

Corning Meat

Cut lean raw beef into large pieces and remove all fat. Place in sterile canning jars and cover with a strong brine solution made of 1 cup salt to 2 quarts water. Just screw on regular seals and lids on the jars. Meat should last up to one year, but it will become saltier and tougher with time. Before using, soak the meat in fresh water up to 24 hours and change the water a couple of times. To tenderize, add 1 Tbsp. of vinegar to the cooking water.

Preserving Bread

Bake or buy bread uncut and whole. Rub it with vinegar and store in a cool, dry place. Tupperware bread boxes make good containers and provide a good seal. Zip bags will also work. Preserved bread should last for many days.

Preserving Eggs

If possible buy farm fresh (un-refrigerated) eggs. If eggs have been refrigerated, allow them to warm to room temperature before coating them.

Coated Eggs: Coat each egg with Vaseline, solid shortening, or dip it in melted paraffin. After coating, store in original plastic or styrofoam containers. Turn the containers over each week to keep the yokes suspended. Coated eggs will last four to six weeks.

Salted Eggs: To keep eggs four to six months, place them in a large jar and cover with a strong brine solution of 1 cup salt to 2 quarts water. Leave no air space. Seal and stow in a cool, dark place. The yokes will turn reddish color and eggs become salty, but they are delicious when hard boiled. When removing salted eggs from the jar, fill up the empty space in the jar with fresh water.

Water-glass Eggs: To preserve eggs an amazing six months without refrigeration, submerge them in a large jar filled with a solution made from 1 part sodium silicate to 10 parts cool fresh water. The only downside when preserved this way is that the egg whites can't be whipped. You can buy sodium silicate from any chemical supply house. Use the powered form. It costs about $15 for five pounds.

Drying Coconuts

If you're cruising in the tropics where there is an abundance of coconuts, try this. It is a simple and easy method for preserving this nutritious food. After removing the white coconut meat from the hard shell, coarsely grate the meat. Place the grated meat in a roasting pan and bake at 200° F for two hours. Toss it frequently until it is dry and golden brown. After cooling, store in airtight containers. It should last for several months.

Preparing coconut meat (copra) for drying under the Polynesian sun.

Storing Lemon and Lime Juice

Citrus fruits are frequently abundant when sailing in the tropics. Squeeze lemons or limes and fill sterilized jars (lids too) with the fresh juice. Dissolve one aspirin per pint of juice in each jar. Cap and shake well. Juices will keep several months.

Flag Etiquette

There are no legal requirements governing the display of flags aboard cruising boats. But the proper flying of flags is established by long marine tradition. Failure to follow that tradition marks the mariner either as a careless or an unknowing skipper. Many cruising boats fail to display their flags properly.

Flag Display—Sailboats

While underway on a U. S. cruising sailboat, either the national ensign (50 stars in a field) or the yacht ensign (13 stars in a circle) are properly displayed in only two positions: 1) on a stern staff, or 2) two-thirds of the way up the leech of the aftermost sail on Marconi-rigged boats. If the aftermost sail is gaff rigged, the ensign is flown at the highest point of the sail where it meets the gaff. On gaff rigs, this is generally accomplished with a special flag halyard designed for the purpose. In international waters the national ensign is preferable to the yacht ensign because of its more universal recognition.

It is improper to fly any U.S. colors (national ensign or yacht ensign) on flag halyards from either the port or starboard spreaders. When at anchor, the only correct position for the U. S. ensign is on a stern staff. Though it's unofficial, many cruisers attach it (somewhat incorrectly) to the backstay at about eye level.

While underway, the U. S. ensign can be flown 24 hours a day—but can be lowered when sailing alone offshore. At anchor, the ensign should be displayed only between 0800 and sunset.

Wrong dislplay of ensign.

Flag Display—Powerboats

On U. S. cruising powerboats, display the ensign on a stern staff and the courtesy flag on the starboard spreader if the boat carries a signal mast. Otherwise the courtesy flag must be displayed from a staff at the bow.

Wrong also.

Correctly displayed ensign.

National Courtesy Flags

The flag of the country you're visiting is called the courtesy flag. It is properly flown only from the starboard spreader and remains flying day and night while you are in that country's waters. Most correctly, only one flag at a time should be flown from your flag halyard—though commonly other flags are sometimes displayed below it. (Do not fly any other national flags under the courtesy flag.)

Quarantine Flag

The yellow international "Q-flag" or quarantine flag is flown on the starboard spreader when entering a foreign port or when returning to a U.S. port from a foreign country. It signals that the vessel is free of contagious disease and requests clearance into that country. After you've completed the clearance formalities, the quarantine flag is replaced by the proper courtesy flag at the starboard spreader. When arriving at a new port of entry, small cruising boats frequently dispense with the Q-flag, choosing to fly the new country's courtesy flag instead. However, in some places this shortcut may be challenged.

Flag Size

Tradition also dictates the appropriate size for flags displayed at sea. Flags are sold in standardized sizes, but here are the recommendations: The national or yacht ensign should approximate one inch on the *fly* (horizontal measurement) for each foot of the boat's length. I think that's larger than most cruising boats display. The *hoist* (vertical measurement) should be two-thirds of the fly. All other flags should be one size smaller than the U.S. ensign.

Distress Flag

Though not official, the U.S. ensign displayed upside down is considered to be a signal of distress.

Ditch Bags (Abandon-Ship Bags)

The following list contains elements of two different survival kits assembled for extended cruising on large sailboats, offered here as a guide to help you assemble your own abandon-ship survival kit. Modify it for your own needs and intended cruising. (The author is indebted to the schooner Endurance, Captain Marv Miller, and to the sloop Victoria, Captain Jeff Thompson, for sharing this information.)

The contents of the kit that have to stay dry should be either shrink-wrapped or packaged in reusable zip bags. The whole kit should be stowed aboard in a readily accessible location. River rafting bags would work well and provide the necessary waterproofing; check at camping stores. To each bag, attach flotation such as a life vest to keep it buoyant plus a brightly colored 30-foot length of polypropylene line, which also floats. Smaller boats will be able to take only a portion of the following list of equipment and supplies.

Equipment

Waterproof flashlight (2D) and extra batteries
Flashlight (AA) Maglite
Duct tape—one roll
6 Cyalume light sticks
Cutting board—1/8" plywood (12"x12")
Butane lighter
Can opener with bottle-top opener—stainless steel
Plastic containers, various sizes with lids
2 Collapsible cups
Emery cloth—for striking matches and sharpening hooks
Small funnel
Hacksaw blade
Plastic through-hull ½" with SS washers to make rain catcher
Plastic tarp—5'-7' to make rain catcher
6 feet nylon hose—1/2" to make rain catcher

2 Folding plastic water jugs—5 gallons each
Life raft repair kit and patch kit
Silicone sealant—1 tube
6 Sailmaker's needles—SS, large and small
1 Spool waxed sailmaker's heavy thread
Line—5'x ¼"
Line—10'x 1/8"
Line—100'x 3/8" - w/thimble & snap-shackle for sea anchor
Sea anchor
Waterproof matches
2 Knives—6" fishing knives in sheaths
Knife—Swiss Army
Sharpening stone
Underwater Epoxy
Finger saw—w/finger rings
Scissors, blunt tip
Screwdriver—w/multi tips
Pliers
Wire cutters
Solar stills—2 for making water
4 Large sponges
2 Towels
Watermaker, PUR Survivor 06
Watermaker biocide
2 Whistles on lanyards
Zip bags, assorted
Pencils and paper
Photocopies of all important papers
$50 in one-dollar bills
Duplicate credit card

Medical

Vitamin pills
Seasick pills
Sun Block, waterproof
Hydrogen Peroxide
Aloe vera lotion
Betadine (first-aid antibiotic)
Kaopectate
Surgical tape, waterproof
Vasoline

Tweezers
Zinc oxide
Aspirin
Gauze—4" x 4 yards
Lip ice

Rescue Aids

2 Flares—smoke
3 Flares—red hand-held
3 Red hand-held SOLAS MK6
6 Flares—parachute
Air Horn
EPIRB
Radar reflector—life raft
Signaling mirrors
2 Water dye markers—orange
VHF—hand-held w/replaceable batteries
Orange signaling flag—2' x 2'
Personal strobe lights

Navigation Aids

Pilot Charts for oceans you're cruising
Hand-held compass
Dividers
Quartz watch

Food and Water

Bouillon cubes—chicken/beef
Hard candy—(glucose)
Raisins
High-energy food bars
Five gallons water from retrieved Jerry Jugs

Personal Equipment

Book—*Survivor* by Michael Greenwald
Book—*Captain's Guide to Life Raft Survival*
Candle
Dark glasses and prescription glasses
Hats—wide brim

Inflatable life vests
Long pants and long-sleeved shirtsPolar blankets
Capalene underwear
Log book
Salt-water soap
Tooth brush
Toilet paper in zip bag

Fishing Gear

Fish hooks—small & large, single & treble
Fishing gaff—folding
Fishing line—80#
Gloves
Yarn—bright colors for lures
Fishing lures
Needle-nosed pliers
Swivels—40# and 80#
Wire leader
Hand reel
Sinkers
Spear gun or Hawaiian sling

Acquiring Drugs, Medicines, and Supplies

This listing was developed from several medical kits prepared for extended offshore cruises. Again, my thanks to the schooner Endurance and the sloop Victoria. Use it to organize and plan your own medical kit. Confer with your own personal physician for specific recommendations, dosages, and prescriptions. It contains basic drugs as well as personal medicines the individual cruiser might require. It also includes medicines specific to cruising areas where exposure to certain medical risks are well known. An example of this is Aralen (chloroquine phosphate), an anti-malarial drug.

The cruiser is responsible for his or her selection of personal drugs and medicines, which should be supported by opinions of competent medical professionals of their own choosing.

Prescription Drugs	Usage
Acetaminophen w/codeine (Tylenol #3)	pain
Ampicillin, 250 mg cap	antibiotic, broad spectrum
Aralen (chloroquine phosphate)	anti-malarial
Auralgan Otic	dear drops—pain
Bactrim-400(Sulfamethoxazole) 80 mm tabs	antibacterial
Lidocaine 1%	local anesthetic
Cloxacillin sodium 250 mg	antibiotic, broad spectrum
Compazine suppository 25 mg	sea sickness
Decadron (dexamethasone)	corticosteroid
Donnatal	intestine cramps
Epinephrine - injection 1 ml	acute allergic reaction
Ergostat 2 mg SL tablets	migraine
Erythromycin 250 mg caps	antibacterial
Inderal	beta blocker
Keflex (cephalexin) 250 mg	antibiotic
Lasix (furosemide)	diuretic
Imodium AD	anti-diarrhea
Macrodantin 50 mg cap	bladder infections
Mannitol 20%	ciguatera (fish) poisoning
Otocort Otic	ear drops—infection
Penicillin VK 250 mg tab	antibiotic
Phenergan (promethazine) 25mg	antihistamine
Phenobarbital 15 mg	anticonvulsant
Polymox (amoxicillin) 250 mg	antibiotic broad spectrum
Selsun 2 1/2 % shampoo	skin yeast
Silvadene 1% cream 400 gr.	burn ointment
Talwin Nx	pain
Transderm-Scop 1.5 mg/72hr patches	sea sickness
Valium (diazepam)	anti-anxiety
Velosef (cephradine)	antibiotic
Vosol Otic	ear drops

Over-the-Counter Medicines	Usage
A&D ointment	skin/sunburn/insects
Adolph's Tenderizer papain) 3.5 oz	jellyfish stings/insect bites
Ammonia	jellyfish stings
Aspirin	pain
Avon Skin-So-Soft	no-see-um (sand fly) repellent
Boric acid power	kills roaches
Cavit 0.7 oz tube	temp tooth filling
Calamine lotion	skin
Chlorine bleach	coral cuts
Digel tabs	antacid
Dramamine/Bonine	sea sickness
Epson salt—1 pound	sprain soaking/enemas
Extend 12- hour liquid	cough syrup
Kaopectate 8 oz	diarrhea

Neosporin cream	skin
Pepto Bismol	upset stomach
Providone iodine solution—8 oz	disinfectant
Robitussin liquid	cough syrup
Stugeron-(not avail. in U.S.)	sea sickness
Tinactin (toinaftate)	fungus
Triaminic tabs	decongestant
Tums tabs	antacid
Tylenol	pain
Vitamin C—500 mg tabs	supplement

Medical Supplies

Ace elastic bandage—3" x 5 yds.
Arm sling—medium
Band-Aids—various sizes
Butterfly closures—medium
Inflatable cast
Cotton balls
Micropore tape—1" x 10 yds.
Micropore tape—1/2" x 5 yds.
Gauze pads—2" x 3"
Gauze pads – 4" x 4"
Q-Tips
Rolled gauze—1" x 7 yds.
Rolled gauze—2 x 5 yds.
Wrapping—3" x 4 yds.

Medical Instruments

Bulb syringe—3 oz
Sterile dispos. rubber gloves
Magnifying glass
Needles—21 ga. 1 ½"
Olsen-Hager needle holder
Scissors
Splinter forceps—tweezers
Sutures—nylon
Sutures—silk
Syringe/needles—5/8"-3 cc
Thermometer
Tweezers

The following information and medical listings borrow from Dr. Don McGillis' excellent *Medicine-At-Sea* course, which was taught for many years at Orange Coast College, Costa Mesa, CA. Dr. Don sent hundreds of cruisers "down-to-the-sea" well prepared for the medical demands of blue-water cruising.

This list is basic and should be supplemented with the cruiser's own personal medications and any necessary supplies to meet the medical requirements of the crew. It should also be modified to reflect the specific medical demands of the cruising areas to be visited, i.e. anti-malarial medicines in the tropics, etc. In all cases, consult with your personal physician when assembling your own ship's medical supplies.

Ship's Medical Kit

Oral Medications	Usual Dosage
Ampicillin 250mg. caps (or Amoxicillin 250mg).	1 or 2 q 6h
Aspirin 5mg	1 or 2 q 3h prn pain or fever
Bactrim	QID
Benadryl 25mg. caps	1 or 2 q 4h prn
Ephedrine 25mg. caps	1 q 4h
Erythromycin (use if allergic to penicillin)	250 - 500 mg q 6h
Imodium AD	1 initial. then 1 q wet BM
Lasix 40mg. tablets	20-40mg. p.o /10-20mg. I..M.
Maalox—liquid and tablets (antacid)	1 oz prn
Tetracycline 250mg. caps (or Doxycycline 100mg.)	1 or 2 q 6h

Injectable Drugs	Usual Dosage
Benadryl 10mg./cc	25-50 mg q 4 to 6h
Dexamethasone 4mg./cc	1 or 2 cc q 6 to 48h
Demerol 50mg./cc	1 or 2 cc q 3h
Epinephrine 1:1000	¼ to ½ e 2h
Lidocaine 1%	locally prn

Topical Medications	Usual Dosage
Caladryl Lotion	prn
Neoploycin ointment	apply TID prn
Providone scrub	prn
Sun screen	prn
Sodium sulamyd 10 ophthalmic solution	1 drop in eye q 2h
Tincture of Benzoin	makes tape stick better
Uval	prn
Vioform HC cream	apply TID prn
Vosol HC otic drops	3 or 4 drops in affected ear qd

Medical Supplies

2", 3", & 4" elastic bandages
4" x 4" gauze squares (in sterile packages of 10)
Adhesive tape ¼", ½", 1", 2"
Kling bandage 2" & 4"
Syringes & needles:
- 3cc w/ 25 ga. 5/8" needle
- 3cc w/22 ga. 1" needle
- 10cc w/18 ga. 1 ½" needle

Enema syringe
Ear syringe
Air Splints (inflatable cast)
Cotton cast padding
Cotton balls & 4.0 nylon sutures with cutting needles

Steristrips 1/8” and ¼”
Q-Tips
Thermometer
Alcohol sponges
Band-Aids
Resuscitube

Medical Instruments

Needle holder with scissors
Skin forceps
Splinter forceps
2 hemostats
Scissors
Jeweler’s loop (magnifying glass)

Pharmacy and Medical Abbreviations

Pharmacy Abbreviations

q	each or every
h	hour/hours
qd	each day
prn	as needed
hs	hours sleep
p.o.	by mouth
pc	after meals (post cibum
ac	before meals (ante cibum)
gtts	drops
mg/s	millegram/s
gm/s	gram/s
gr/s	grain/s
cc	cubic centimeters
sig:	directions
BID	2 times daily
TID	3 times daily
QID	4 times daily

Medical Abbreviations and Vocabulary

C.N.S.	Central Nervous System
G.I.	Gastro-Intestinal
G.U.	Genito-Urinary
I.M.	IntraMuscular
I.V.	Intravenous
M.I.	Myocardial Infarction (reduction of blood)
P.O.	By mouth
Febrile	Fever
Hyper-	Over or above normal
Hypo-	Under or below normal

Ischemia	Reduced blood supply
Purulent	Pus containing
Systemic	Throughout the system

Pediatric Doses (for antibiotics, use the smaller adult dosage)

3 to 4 years	¼ adult dose
5 t0 6 years	1/3 adult dose
7 to 9 years	½ adult dose
10 to 12 years	2/3 adult dose

Drug and Medicine Descriptions

Ampicillin	A broad spectrum antibiotic. Good for many different infections.
Amoxicillin	Same as Ampicillin above. Same dosage.
Aspirin	For pain and fever. Also use prophylactically to reduce blood clot tendency. Buffered aspirin is tolerated better in the stomach.
Atropine	A very strong heart stimulant and gastro-intestinal sedative. Injectable 1/150 gr./cc.
Azo-Gantrisin	An azo dye and sulfa combination for urinary tract infections. Turns urine orange to red. Take 2 tablets 4 times a day with lots of water.
Bactrim	Antibacterial sulfa drug. Good for urinary and middle ear infections.
Benadryl	25mg & 50mg capsules. An antihistamine that is excellent for allergic reactions, sea sickness and as a sedative. For sedation and allergy. To maintain alertness, give alone, ephedrine 25mg. with it.
Caladryl Lotion	Apply to skin for rash and itching.
Demerol	A strong synthetic narcotic for severe pain.
Doxycycline	Broad spectrum antibiotic. Good for traveler's diarrhea. Can be taken (prophylactically) in anticipation of exposure.
Empirin/Codeine	A pain reliever stronger that aspirin but tending to induce nausea. 1-2 tablets every 3 hours.
Ephedrine	A central nervous system stimulant. An upper. Improves breathing. Raises pulse and blood pressure.

Epinephrine	An extremely potent hormone stimulant. For severe allergic reactions and shock.
Erythromycin	A broad spectrum antibiotic. Used for upper-respiratory infections. Also used for persons allergic to penicillin. Specific to Legionnaire's Disease.
Imodium	An anti-diarrheal, but safer than Lomitil. Fast and long lasting.
Lasix	A potent, short acting diuretic (removes water from bloodstream). Used for edema (swelling) and after near drowning in salt water.
Lidocaine	(Xylocaine) 1%. A local anesthetic. Inject directly into tissue.
Lotrimin Cream	1%. A topical anti-fungal cream.
Maalox	An antacid that's made with milk of magnesia. For sour stomach, heartburn, and as a laxative.
Mannitol	Administered intravenously for ciguatera (fish) poisoning.
Morphine Sulfate	¼ gr./cc. For severe pain. A very potent narcotic analgesic. Stops intestinal muscular activity, thus causing constipation. Used for kidney stones, fractures, heart attack. Morphine is a strong respiratory depressant and is very addicting.
Neopolycin Ointment	Three antibiotics in a Vaseline base. Good for abrasion and burns.
Phenobarbital	A long-acting sedative. Addicting.
Providone Soap	(Betadine). Antiseptic scrub solution containing iodine.
Sodium Sulamyd 10%	A sulfa containing eye drop for eye infections.
Tincture of Benzoin	Alcohol-based paint to apply to skin prior to taping or using Steristrips. Makes tape stick better. Protects the skin. Do not get in open wounds.
Tetracycline	A broad-spectrum antibiotic that is specific for most contamination-caused bowel infections. Good for many infections. Can cause hypersensitivity to sun. Don't drink milk while taking. Can be used prophylactically while traveling to prevent diarrhea.
Uval Lotion	A sunscreen lotion.

Vioform HC Cream	An anti-infective, anti-fungal and anti-inflammatory cream.
Vosol Otic HC	Anesthetic ear drops good for swimmer's ear. You may also take systemic antibiotics for ear infections.

Dental Supplies *(most available over the counter)*

Small mouth mirror—to see posterior teeth and behind anterior teeth.

Advil, Aleve, Tylenol, aspirin—Get a pain reliever that works for you.

Anbesol or other topical anesthetic—for toothache. Use the gel form and apply with Q-Tip.

Fixodent or other dental adhesive—to temporarily repair or hold in place broken crowns and onlays (large cast restorations).

Petroleum jelly or toothpaste—to temporarily hold in place broken inlays (large cast restorations).

Dycal—a 2-part cement for temporary repair of caps, crowns, and broken teeth (but more permanent than above). Use when professional dental attention will not be available for several days or weeks. (Available only from a dentist.)

Orthodontic wax—to place over the sharp edges of a broken tooth.

Salt packets—Mix with warm water and rinse mouth up to five times daily for bleeding, sore, and/or swollen gum tissue.

Floss—to dislodge anything caught between the teeth.

Hydrogen peroxide—A 50/50 mixture of hydrogen peroxide and water can be used as an oral antimicrobial rinse, but do not swallow. Use only in a 50/50 dilution and only for a short time, such as five days. You can also use it full strength to sterilize crowns and inlays before placing them back into the mouth.

Amoxicillin—a broad-spectrum antibiotic. Can be used for abscesses and other mouth infections. Amoxicillin (prescription) should be in your ship's medical kit.

Chapter 9

Hopefully Helpful Hints

This chapter discusses some commercial products, pieces of equipment, and special procedures that cruising skippers will find helpful.

Products

White vinegar will dissolve deposits that are created when stainless steel and aluminum are exposed in marine environments. It's good on spinnaker-pole pistons and to keep hinges on ports and hatches from seizing up.

Muriatic acid will dissolve calcium carbonate deposits in marine heads and hoses. It cleans out your engine heat exchangers, which might solve your overheating problems. Rust from non-aluminum parts and tools can be removed by immersion. Muriatic acid removes zinc pencils from nut holders. It's fast and potent when used full strength. When diluting, always pour the acid into the water—not vice versa. Wear rubber gloves and safety glasses.

To use muriatic acid as a preventative measure on your boat's head, mix one pint of acid and two gallons of either fresh or salt water. Pour the solution into the head and pump the bowl dry. Follow this with a gallon of plain water and pump dry, but don't pump the solution out of the system. Now, allow about 45 minutes for the mix to work. It will dissolve the buildup of calcium carbonate in the discharge hose.

On our boat the worst deposits were always nearest the through-hull fitting—where the head discharge meets the salt water. The calcium carbonate will eventually completely seal off your hose and through-hull fitting, but the muriatic acid will clear and clean them without damage. If you have reason to remove the discharge hose, you can also break up the deposits by banging the hose on the side of the boat to clear the hose without resorting to the acid. For sever clogs, repeat the process immediately and then practice preventative maintenance every 4 to 6 months. If you have problems or questions, you can call Mike Sheppard, head of the Service Department, at Raritan Engineering at 609-825-4900.

If you've used muriatic acid full strength on a project, when finished let the acid stand until it clears. It can then be saved for reuse. Put a gallon on board before you leave. You can buy it at any hardware store.

Blaster is the very best penetrant and corrosion buster I've found for boats. It can free and lubricate stuck parts that nothing else seems to touch. Blaster Div. of W.K.W. Co., Garfield Heights, OH 44125.

Lime Away If you have a stubborn overheating problem and your engine is fresh water cooled, try adding a gallon of Lime Away to the cooling system. Run the engine for about 45 minutes and drain. This will dissolve the mineral deposits that form within the block and reduce engine cooling capacity. Sometimes you can solve heat problems that have resisted all other attempts.

Corrosion Block is an excellent penetrant and light lubricant that often works where other products fail when you're trying to free seized-up equipment.

Boeshield, **STP 3**, and **Lanocote** are useful for protecting equipment inside and out. These products leave a lasting film on all metal surfaces that resists marine exposure.

303 or **Armor All** are good for protecting all kinds of rubber, leather, and plastic fittings that constantly get exposed to the sun, and to extend their life. Use it on inflatable dinghies, jerry jugs (especially their caps), turnbuckle boots, dinghy fuel hoses, rubber seals on your ports and hatches, and so forth. We didn't use it on our dodger's vinyl windows, but I think it might work there too—carefully test it on a small area first. TruValue hardware stores carry these products. You can also use silicon spray for rubber protection and silicon paste for O-rings. TruValue carries these also.

Equipment

Small brass padlocks —all keyed alike—will come in handy for lots of things, so take along a dozen of them. They can secure all your hatches, your dinghy, equipment stored on deck, etc. And all with the same key.

If you install an **inverter** (at least 600 watts) onboard, you can use small power tools when necessary. I frequently needed and used a **3/8" drill** and **saber saw**. You can charge all those small battery-powered appliançes, too, or use them directly on 115 volts. Take **sharp bits** that can handle stainless steel. They will come in handy.

Take two to four **extra snatch blocks**. These can be used for a number of things—extra mooring lines, kedging off when aground, going aloft, and changing jib sheets.

You'll need some way to climb the mast. A **boatswain's chair** is the easiest way up there. Use any halyard and lead it to the anchor windlass if you can. Use a snatch block tied off to a mooring cleat to get the correct angle for the windlass.

You'll need a boatswain's chair or some other way to get up the mast.

Some people swear by their **mast steps**, and they work well for single-handers. (I'm not a mast-step fan because they foul sheets and create extra windage.)

Install a **weed cutter** to protect your propeller from nets, fish line, and from wrapping an anchor line. Any of these situations could severely damage your running gear and even threaten the safety of your vessel. The unit mounts on the propeller and will cut any lines that threaten to wrap the shaft and disable the vessel. Call Spurs, Ft. Lauderdale, to get a brochure, or buy direct (Spurs-Line and Weed Cutter, Ft. Lauderdale, FL 305-463-2707).

Assemble a kit of **fastenings**—nuts, bolts, screws, washers, clevis pins, shackles, cotter pins, and on and on. Make sure it's all stainless steel.

Assemble a kit of **plumbing fittings**—brass fittings, washers, and replacement hoses. And take lots of **hose clamps** of various sizes—only the ones that are totally stainless, including the tightening bolt.

Assemble a kit of **electrical fittings**—extra wire of various sizes, fittings, switches, a crimping tool, shrink wrap, solder and a soldering iron.

Assemble a kit of **sail repair materials**—thread, bees wax, palm and needles, sail patch material, sticky-back materials.

Buy a **broad tip** for your **soldering iron** so you can do marlinspike and splicing projects onboard. Your inverter will provide 110 volts, just like ashore.

Install a **bilge alarm** to alert you to rising water. Lots of skippers have gone below to find water over the floor boards as their first indication of trouble. Don't rely on your automatic bilge pump to handle every situation. You need an early-warning system to sound while you still have time to find the problem.

Procedures

Double clamp all hose fittings that are below the waterline and inspect them regularly. Replace rusted clamps immediately.

Go aloft before every extended passage. Check everything and lubricate the halyard sheaves. Check your anchor light. While you're at it, wipe down the sail track and use of bit of spray Teflon on it as you come down. Watch what happens the next time you drop the mainsail—like a rock!

Check and maintain your sea cocks. They should work easily by hand, so exercise them frequently. A seized-up sea cock could cost you your boat—or worse. They should be checked and serviced each time you haul out. Teach the first mate their locations and operation.

When underway, **check your running rigging** every day for chafe. End-for-ending your sheets and halyards can double their life expectancy—and save your cruising kitty.

Chapter 10

Contact Information

These references are offered as a source of information and expertise in your search for answers to supplying, outfitting, and provisioning questions.

Amateur Radio

American Radio Relay League—ARRL
800-326-3952
Source for amateur radio and licensing information.

Gordon West Radio School
2414 College Dr., Costa Mesa, CA 92626
714-549-5000, 714-434-0666 Fax
Books, tapes, classes for amateur radio licensing; some tapes are available at Radio Shack. Call for others.

Communications and Navigation

AT&T High Seas Radiotelephone Service, 800-SEA-CALL
AT&T High Seas Direct call 800-392-2067
Register before departure to avoid giving your credit card number over the air.

Comsat Mobile Communications
22300 Comsat Dr., Clarksburg, MD 20871
800-685-7898

Provides the communications link to Inmarsat-C satellites, communications, and e-mail.

Magellan Systems Corp.
960 Overland Court, San Dimas, CA 91773
909-394-5000
Satellite Navigation and Communication. Makes full line of GPS and communication equipment. Just released a new e-mail satellite system and global phone system.

PinOak Digital Corp.
P.O. Box 360, Gladstone, NJ 07934
800-PINOAK-1
Makes communication equipment that provides e-mail communications and private WX reports.

Software Systems Consulting
615 S. El Camino Real, San Clemente, CA 92672
714-498-5784
Equipment and software for gathering weather and sending e-mail from offshore.

Trimble Navigation Ltd.
3400 188th Street SW, Suite 535, Lynnwood, WA 98037-6722
800-874-6722
Builds the electronics to access Inmarsat-C satellite communications.

Insurance

Blue Water Insurance
Jupiter, FL
800-866-8906
Cruising insurance—all oceans. Discount to SSCA members.
They can also write cruisers' medical coverage.

Boat/U.S. Insurance 800-283-2883
Boat insurance—U.S. and Caribbean waters.

Lloyds of London
World-wide marine insurance coverage—written by many U.S. insurance brokers and Blue Water Insurance above.

West Marine Insurance
800-937-8895
Boat insurance—U.S. and limited Mexican waters. No Bahamian or Caribbean coverage.

Medical

Costa Mesa Pharmacy, % Robert Quint
Costa Mesa, CA
714-642-0106
Scopolamine gel—until patches are back. Seasick preventative requires a prescription from a doctor (5 to 10 applications, $12.) Rub into wrist or behind ear; good for eight to 12 hours.

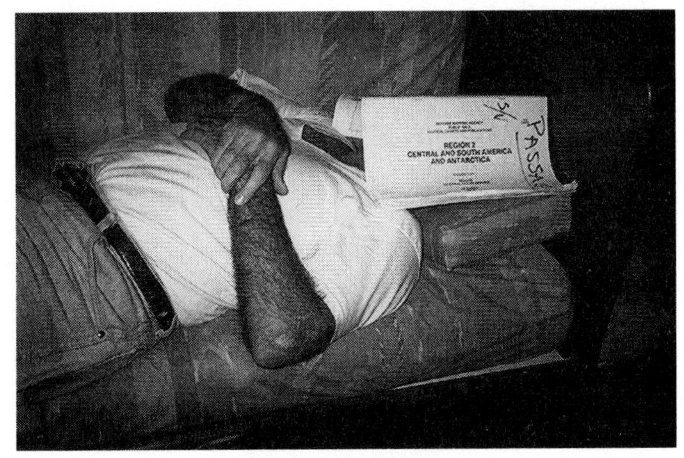

Sleep-study technique.

Panorama Pharmacy
% Earl Broidy
Los Angeles, CA
800-247-9767
Scopolamine gel for sea sickness, needs a prescription.

International Academy of Compounding Pharmacists
Houston, TX
800-927-4227
Call for the nearest compounding pharmacist for Scopolamine gel. They list all compounding druggists in U.S.

Hawaii Chemteck International, Pacific Center
P.O. Box 92015, Pasadena, CA 91109
818-568-8606
Is developing a test kit for ciguatera fish poisoning.

Organizations

Seven Seas Cruising Association,
1525 South Andrews, Suite 217, Ft. Lauderdale, FL 33316
954-463-2431
SSCA—worldwide. This non-commercial association of cruising sailors publishes a 50-page monthly newsletter and an annual equipment survey.

Marine Resource Materials

Cruising Ports: Florida to California via Panama (3rd edition) - John Rains
Point Loma Publishing
P.O. Box 60190, San Diego, CA 92166
888-302-2628
Cruising guide to ports between the U.S. coasts via the Panama Canal. Lots of information for cruisers.

Cruiser's Radio Guide (2nd edition) - Roger Krautkremer
FMS Services, 2539 S. Fairplay Way, Aurora, CO 80014
Call 303-695-8715
Complete guide to licensing, installation, marine radio services, adn maritime mobile operations. This great little book should be on board any boat with a marine radio. Condenses information found in many other locations. A "must have" resource book.

Lightning and Boats - by Michael V. Huck Jr., published by Seaworthy Publications, 1995. Excellent discussion of all aspects of lightning as it relates to small boats.

U.S.C.G. Boating Safety Hotline: 800-368-5647
Marine Federal Requirements—navigation lights, Rules of the Road, and aids to navigation. Request literature.

Raritan Engineering, NJ 609-825-4900. If you have head or marine sanitation problems, ask for Mike Sheppard; he's head of the Service Dept. and very knowledgeable.

Schools

Calvert School
105 Tuscany Road, Baltimore, MD 21210
410-243-6030
Correspondence school; K through 8th grade for cruising kids. First-class schooling.

Gordon West Radio School
714-549-5000
Gordon offers courses, tapes, and books for amateur radio license preparation. Books are available at Radio Shack stores.

Supplies and Equipment

Hasse—Petrick Sails
Point Hudson, Port Townsend, WA 98368
260-385-1640
This all-girl sail loft makes outstanding sails for cruisers.

Christine Davis Flags
923 S.E. 20th St., Ft. Lauderdale, FL 33316
954-527-1605
Courtesy Flags; makes excellent and reasonable flags for all countries; they will ship to you.

Custom Marine Fabrication
5286 Industrial Dr., Huntington Beach, CA
714-891-9050
Makes excellent tanks and marine fabrications. Ask for Jim or John.

Counter Assault
P.O. Box 4721, Dept. R, Missoula, MT 59806
800-695-3394
Pepper Spray—made for grizzly bears, 15- to 25-foot range. Several sizes for both vessel and personal protection.

Evert-Fresh Bags
P.O. Box 540974, Houston, TX 77254-0974
800-822-8141
Special plastic bags for fruits and vegetables that retard ripening. Greatly extends the life of fresh produce three to 10 times. Use with or without refrigeration.

Evert-Fresh bags will extend the life of fruits and vegetables several times over.

Heart Interface
21440 68th Ave. S, Kent, WA 98032
800-446-6180
Makes inverters, chargers, controls, instrumentation, and TankTender gauges for multiple tanks. Quality equipment.

Idea Development Company
83 Idea Place, Sequim, WA 98382
360-683-3000
Makes *Wheel-a-Weigh* dinghy wheels with large 16-inch tires. Requires pin insertion to deploy. These wheels are deep enough to protect standard length 8- to 15-HP outboards. Order model WR-16-I, $150.

Inflatable Boats of Florida
2601 Overseas Hwy., Marathon, FL 33050
305-743-7085
Sells dinghy wheels as noted in text.

Jade Mountain
P.O. Box 4616
Boulder, CO 80306
800-442-1972
Non-boating source for lots of 12-volt equipment including solar panels, wind generators; good prices. Call for big catalogue and technical information.

Kern's Sails
1781 Whittier, Costa Mesa, CA
714-645-7741
Cruisers' sailmaker, small loft, makes bullet-proof sails; excellent service and prices.

PUR Watermakers
9300 North 75th Avenue
Minneapolis, MN 55428
800-787-5463 (information and tech support)
Makes best-selling 12- and 24-volt watermakers for cruisers. Good product support.

Real Goods
555 Leslie Street
Ukiah, CA 95482
800-994-4243 customer service, 800-919-2400 technical service. Non-boating source for 12-volt equipment such as solar panels, wind generators, inverters, excellent prices. Call for catalogue and special membership discounts.

Recreational Industries
P.O. Box 1840, Clackamas, OR 97015
503-655-9443
Manufactures Flip-Up dinghy wheels, allows beach landings with your tender. The 10" wheels are shorter than 16" models above, but more convenient. Try asking for bigger wheels. Measure to make sure they will protect your dinghy prop when beach landing. Order model 2200-10 at $159, plus (recommended) $15.95 for salt-water kit.

Scanmar International
432 S. First Street, Richmond, CA 94804
510-215-5505
Factory direct wind vanes, including the high rated Monitor and other models.

Spurs Line and Weed Cutters
Ft. Lauderdale, FL
305-463-2707
Make a cutting device mounted on prop shaft designed for owner installation. Protects the vessel's propeller from lines and nets. Great for peace of mind.

SHURflo Pumps
12650 Westminster Ave., Santa Ana, CA 92706-2100
800-854-3218
SHURflo makes a full line of top quality marine pumps and accessories. They hold up well in cruising situations. Available through West Marine and Boat/US stores.

Trade Wind Inflatables
1720 Pacific Coast Hwy., Huntington Beach, CA
714-960-9003 and 714-960-4373
Sells dinghy wheels as noted in text plus a large selection of inflatables, including Caribs.

Your ideas and opinions are very important to us. Please complete this form and mail it back. Thanks.

Passagemaker Publications
P.O. Box 359
Seal Beach, CA 90740

Errors and Corrections

Walt, I found an error in All About Cruising! Please correct it.
Chapter _______ Page _______ Paragraph ______ Line ______
It says ____
____
and it should say ____
____
____

Comments

Walt, here's an update about your information found in
Chapter _______ Page _______ Paragraph ______ Line ______
____
____
____
____
____
____

(Remarks on the back)

Remarks

Walt, here's some great information for your next edition of All About Cruising:

____
____
____
____
____
____
____

Walt, please include more information about the following topics in your next edition of All About Cruising:

____
____
____
____
____
____
____

Regards from,

Name ____________________________ Date ______________
Boat name ______________________(power/sail) _Size _________
Address ____
Home port ____
Phone ____________________________Call sign _____________
Home cruising waters __________________________________